T0148617

Conquering The Marathon

HALF TO WHOLE...BEGINNER TO ADVANCED

Lynn Gray, M.S.
RRCA Certified Coach

authorHOUSE®

AuthorHouse™
1663 Liberty Drive
Bloomington, IN 47403
www.authorhouse.com
Phone: 1-800-839-8640

© 2012 Lynn Gray. All rights reserved.

No part of this book may be reproduced, stored in a retrieval system, or transmitted by any means without the written permission of the author.

Published by AuthorHouse 12/5/2012

ISBN: 978-1-4772-6107-1 (sc)
ISBN: 978-1-4772-6108-8 (e)

Library of Congress Control Number: 2012915704

Any people depicted in stock imagery provided by Thinkstock are models, and such images are being used for illustrative purposes only. Certain stock imagery © Thinkstock.

This book is printed on acid-free paper.

Because of the dynamic nature of the Internet, any web addresses or links contained in this book may have changed since publication and may no longer be valid. The views expressed in this work are solely those of the author and do not necessarily reflect the views of the publisher, and the publisher hereby disclaims any responsibility for them.

Table of Contents

Phase I
Walk to Walker
Cardio Walking

Phase 2
Walk to Jog
Ratio Training

Phase 3
Jog to Run
Duration Training

Phase 4
Longer to Stronger
Intensity and Stamina

Phase 5
Rest to Race
The Taper

Introduction

The half marathon and marathon distance are comprehensive and challenging goals physically and mentally. I have lived a lifestyle which mirrors long distance training. When I first began running some forty five years ago, the central motivator was for stress release and to be outdoors. Then as distance running became part of my lifestyle, the benefits of becoming more relaxed, having a trim body, gaining new friends, plus the excitement of race events kept me "on the run." The wisdom shared in this book reflects decades of running and lessons learned while training hundreds of walkers and runners of all ages and all physical ability levels. A personal motivation is to share the knowledge gained from my journey as a walker to a runner plus the countless experiences of others who have taken up the "walk to run" challenge.

Distance event opportunities ranging from 5Ks to half and whole marathons have grown for men and women of all fitness levels. A big reason for growth is the simplicity of this sport. Each of us can go out the door any time to run or walk for an hour. During the hour we improve our minds with relaxing thoughts and improve our bodies by using just about every muscle in our body. For men and women who are weight conscious, a vigorous cardio walk or running speeds up metabolism for the rest of the day.

Each of you will take take up the long distance challenge for different reasons. The outcomes of training toward your fitness goal will affect the rest of your life. Putting yourself on the line and engaging in total aerobic conditioning for a finite distance and specific time goal is both exciting and empowering. Increased self-esteem, decreased body fat, less stress, quality friendship, and an improved lifestyle are but a few of the results experienced while becoming the fittest person you can be.

The distance is nothing; it is only the first step that is difficult. Mme. Deffand

Forward Movement Thinking

I define forward movement as walking, jogging, and running. This book is based on the premise that walkers and joggers alike can become runners if physical adaptation is developed gradually. Before *one can run a mile, they need to first be able to vigorously walk a mile*. Likewise, before one can *move fast they must learn to first move slow*. Forward movement is as simple as that.

Those above statements reflect the necessary physical adaptation the body needs before impact. The faster the body moves forward, the quicker the body mechanics such as joint and muscle alignment must react and function smoothly. Most of us do not think of taking a walk or a run as an injury prone sport, nor should it be. However, when we jump quickly from the walking movement to running, the amount of impact the body takes is enormous. Gradual training is absolutely vital to avoid needless impact injuries such as shin splints, knee problems, tendonitis, bursitis, and other injuries.

The contents of this book contain extensive physical conditioning and flexibility exercises. Certain muscular exercises are specific to the walk to run movement. A muscular conditioning regiment will help you progress fairly quickly and prevent muscle weaknesses which can lead to injuries. Likewise, daily stretching aimed at those same muscles do wonders to avoid muscle stiffness, soreness, and inflammation. The continual pulling and contracting of the same muscles respond well to specificity stretching exercises which are included in this training manual.

Cross training is an important piece of a complete fitness program. The impact of the walking and/or running movement develops bone density and cardiovascular fitness just to name a few advantages. However, too much impact on the body can result in overstressed joints, muscles, tendons, and ligaments which lead to injuries. Cross training such as swimming, biking, and weight training are excellent components of a fitness regiment which will give the body a "break" from continual impact. Also, cross training will add variety of muscle usage, support recovery, and in general decrease boredom of just participating in one sport.

Nutrition for the active individual is an important component in all physical fitness programs. Whether you desire to lose weight or maintain current weight, eating healthy brings upon a higher level of health. The fitter we become the keener our desire to eat foods which enhance our performance and allow fuel systems to be maintained while in action.

This book is divided into five forward movement phases with both physical preparation and progressive adaptation in mind. Pick and choose the fitness stage you are in. Follow the fitness level schedules provided which match your current ability. Repeat any of the phases until adaptation is reached. Likewise, check your fitness level and readjust according to where you actually are now. There is no official due date to complete the schedules. Each schedule serves as a model for gradual distance fitness leading to the half and/or marathon goal. Runners of all ability levels will enjoy the track and tempo workouts included in the back of this book.

Generally speaking a beginner walker can expect at least a year of training before doing a half marathon or marathon distance with a walk to run ratio. Both beginner and experienced runners can achieve the distance goals with the schedules offered in this book within a year. True of both scenarios is the key consideration: physical adaptation must take place so no injuries occur during the training process.

Within each of the five phases there are informative segments which educate and justify the physical progression being made. A journal for each day of the week is included so you can monitor training and become motivated by the progress made each week and each month. Lastly, all parts are focused on the goal of completing and or competing the half marathon and/or marathon distance.

Phase 1: Walk to Walker
Phase 2: Walk to Jog
Phase 3: Jog to Run
Phase 4: Longer to Stronger
Phase 5: Rest to Race

Where are you now?

Age: _____

Weight: _____ , Measurements: Waist _____ , Hips _____ , Thigh _____

Resting Heart Rate _____ , Maximum Heart Rate _____

What distance can you continually walk, jog, or run currently? _____

What is your average weekly mileage? _____

What is your fastest mile time walking or running? _____

What is your fastest 5K run?_____ What year?_____

What muscle(s) group is weak? _____

What muscle(s) group seems to get tight and inflexible the most?_____

What cross-training do you do? _____ Has it made a difference? _____

The biggest excuse for not working out is? _____

Your meal in the evening is: (circle one)

Small-less than 500 calories, medium-about 800 calories, large-1000+ calories

Goals: examples: weight loss, goal event time (example - 5K in 30 minutes):
2 months _____
4 months _____
6 months _____

Consider what your answers may mean:

* *Resting Heart Rate* - how efficient is your heart pumping blood when not exerting and when exerting. RHR-before getting out of bed is good in the 50's.

* *Maximum Heart Rate* - heart rate goes up with strenuous activity and should go immediately down after a minute of resting. MHR varies with each person and is largely genetic.

* *Current distance is important to note;* a small amount of daily distance (1 mile or so) means start at the beginner level, and conversely a larger distance base means you can begin at the intermediate level or advanced level. In each case it takes time for the body to adapt to impact.

* *Weekly average miles* indicates the body has adapted to distance walking and/or running and can go a longer distance; gradually.

* *How fast can you go?* This is an important cardiorespiratory marker indicating the ability to breathe efficiently despite going faster or the inability to go faster due to less lung capacity.

* *Weak muscle(s) must be strengthened and stretched.* If not, long distance impact could result in injury to the weaker areas.

* *Cross Training exercises should come in this order:* weight training specific for the walking and running movement, biking or spinning which increases leg turnover and swimming which increases lung capacity and adds to agility.

* *Missing workouts generally lead to one of two undesirable results:* making up the missed workout by doubling the next day, or losing the disciplined routine of following the scheduled progressive workouts. In each case, progress will be subtracted and possible injuries of the "doubling of workouts" can occur.

* *Regulating portion control for the evening meal is critical for weight maintenance or weight loss.* Eating small portions during the day and fueling during your exercise time goes a long way in preventing overeating. Generally speaking weight gain results from overeating in the evening due to the slowing down of activity and overall metabolism.

* *Losing weight and initiating a fitness program are two distinct goals.* Losing weight while following an ambitious walk to run program will occur simply by eating a healthy diet and limiting the amount of food in the evening. Maintaining weight and losing weight while training generally occurs. In each case of concern, the body does reshape due to increased muscle and reduction of body fat if the participant routinely follows their distance walking or running program.

Phase I
Walk to Walker

Cardio Walking

Weeks 1 - 8

Workout Weeks 1 – 4
Take a Walk

Level	Intensity per mile	Frequency per week	Distance	Time	Weeks
Beginner walk	17 – 20 min	4 days	2 miles	35 min	1 - 4
Int. beg walk	15 – 16 min	4 days	3 miles	60 min	1 - 4
Adv. beg walk	14 – 15 min	5 days	4 miles	45 min	1 - 4

Below are the progressive training steps to consider as you initiate the first 4 weeks of easy walking.

1. Pick the fitness level which best matches your current physical ability.
2. Intensity means the speed of the walk; easy walking is recommended for the first four weeks for physical adaptation.
3. Develop a sense of pace; time your mile and work towards a 20 minute mile or less.
4. Determine the frequency or total days per week you can engage in the walking workout
5. Record the amount of time per day you can comfortably walk in the journal provided at the end of each schedule.

In the journal also make notations which may include:

a. *Breathing* – easy or challenging; can you talk?
b. *Heart rate* – find your pulse, hold for 15 seconds multiply by 4; rest for one minute and check to see if the heart rate goes down significantly. If not you will need to slow down.
c. *Sweat rate* - ideally you want to sweat so the body can cool
d. *Muscle fatigue* – afterwards is acceptable; during is a sign to shorten the distance until muscle adaptation is met
e. *Intensity* – effort of movement: slow, challenging, or fast
f. *Weather* – humid, cold, hot, etc.
g. *Cross training* - weights, swimming, biking, etc.

Week 1
Walking is Medicine

As our society becomes more focused on technological advances and a busier lifestyle we find ourselves increasingly isolated, stressed, and physiologically more sedentary. The notion of "taking a walking break" is soothing and if practiced, the motion becomes mentally relaxing. Consider "taking a walk" as a far healthier and physically rewarding choice when desiring to briefly detour the stresses of life. It is a fact that the more control we have over our mental and physical well-being, increased overall health will occur, making day to day living more productive and meaningful. Those of us approaching middle age will find many exciting options in the exercise realm and want to be part of the action which a healthy body can deliver. "Taking a walk" will give the muscular and mental medicine needed to be continually mobile and physically independent throughout our lives. Later on as we add a bit of intensity to our walk with cardio walking, and gain aerobic benefits while walking briskly.

There are many gains which walking and brisk walking can give to people of all ages. Consider these following mental and physical perks.

- *Friendship:* Perhaps the greatest walking movement benefit of late is the camaraderie gained from joining walking groups planning a distance goal such as completing a 5K or a half marathon. The largest population gains in distance events are now made up of women. They love conquering new goals and becoming fit while allowing downtime for socializing and relaxing.

- *Mood enhancer:* Regular walking can greatly reduce depression. The ages of sixties, seventies, and beyond reveal an increased sense of isolation and lack of physical and mental stimulation. Retirement, increased isolation from not being in a social environment, and decreased physical health drive the later ages into negative habits often leading to alcoholism and increased drug use. A group walking program resolves this by providing its own social network. The younger ages gain increased self-esteem with an outlet to establish themselves competitively in a physical arena which supports walking and running events. Physiologically exercise increases endorphins, the neurochemicals occurring naturally in the brain which elevate the mood and reduce anxiety levels.`

- *Increased Coordination*: Accidental falls occur more frequently as one allows muscles, balance, and posture to deteriorate. In fact falling accounts for a large number of deaths after 65. The walking movement establishes a continual heel to toe striking gait which aids balance and overall body coordination. The range of motion or leg span of a vigorous cardio walk together with the fast movement of the arms reminds the walker to practice a balanced posture during fast forward movement.

- *Bone Density:* After thirty or so many of us are being reminded to engage in exercises to increase bone density and therefore avoid breaking bones easily. By age 65 one in four women have osteoporosis and have thin bones which look like a honeycomb. From forty on, an increasing number of women get osteopenia, a predecessor to osteoporosis. Many studies have been made which show that the impact of walking, cardio walking and running can slow down and even reverse bone loss by promoting bones to become denser. Lastly, the more muscles we gain surrounding the bones, the more protection our bones and vital organs receive from impact incidents.

- *Get Flexible*: Living out the middle ages and onward reveal a loss of fluidity both in the joints and muscles. The long span required for a full cardio-walk movement requires a stride length of 12 to 16 inches in length which lends itself to leg flexibility. Using the knee as a hinge joint helps with keeping forward movement both fluid and steady on strong knees with well-developed tendons and ligaments. The use of arm propulsion of cardio walking is analogous with the knee/leg movement. In this case the range of motion is established with a full arm swing and assisted with a flexible elbow joint.

- *Up the Metabolism*: The war of the worlds for many of us begins with weight loss vs. weight gain. Let's look at weight gain first. Cardio walking greatly increases the metabolism; the body's ability to burn energy. Conversely, as we age and our appetite decreases, a vigorous walk will stimulate the appetite thereby assuring the important nutrients and minerals to be absorbed into the body. The frosting on the cake for those who desire to lose weight is the development of leg, arm, and core muscle. The increased density of muscle mass increases metabolism even while you are sedentary.

- *Digestive System Relief*: Increase of motion by walking results in a decrease in diabetes due to the body removing sugar from the bloodstream quickly. The intestines are stimulated with vigorous cardio walking. The form needed for cardio walking includes a constant slight swing left and right with the arms which gives the intestines a slight "twisting" effect. This continuous twist will help stimulate bowel movements and in general help rid the body of waste.

- *Breathe Rite!* For sedentary individuals, by age 35 maximal oxygen intakes has decreased by 10%, by 45 it has decreased by 20% or more. Walking increases the efficiency with which the muscle cells take oxygen from the blood, as well as preventing the shrinkage or deterioration of lung tissues. Walking increases oxygen into your lungs. This enables the lungs to handle the increase of air flow more efficiently due to the improved condition of lung tissue and increased development of chest muscles. The lungs become strong, efficient, and work like recharged receivers of air which in turn renew cells while giving the body more energy and preventing normal exertive tasks from leaving you breathless.

- *Heart Rate, where did it go?* As we age blood pressure tends to go up largely due to the arteries becoming less flexible and narrow. Worse yet, those same weakened and narrowing arteries become clogged with cholesterol which can result in heart disease. Cardio walking reduces both a high heart rate and blood pressure due to forcing the narrowing arteries to open up. The increased expansion of the arteries will lessen the work of the heart by lowering its stroke volume and/or pumping. A decrease in resting heart rate and blood pressure become two valuable health markers of the heart working more efficiently. Increased blood flow or circulation due to walking vigorously also helps lessen varicose veins and other related circulatory problems. Physical fatigue lessens as vigorous walking increases, again due to the increase of oxygen and blood circulation.

Week 2
Setting the "Fitness" Table

There are basic steps to follow in a long term fitness program which will provide both motivation and successful progression. Below are basic considerations to get the "job" underway.

1. *Goal Setting:* Each month set a goal; an example would be to complete one mile within 15 min. Another example is to lose two pounds. Other examples include: lower resting heart rate, improve cardio vascular system, strengthen and tone the body. A mid-point goal could be to complete a 5K. Write your event distance goals down, plus other results desired. The contents of each weekly chapter will include a walk to run lesson and a daily journal.

   Goals: examples: weight loss, event time (example - 5K in 35 minutes):
   2 months _____
   4 months _____
   6 months _____
   Year goal _____

2. *Find a Walk to Run Group:* The number one reason for success in long distance walking/running is the camaraderie. The friends made along the way instill positive thinking, accountability, and provide a source of "fitness fun."

3. *The Journal:* Recording one's progress serves as both motivators and teaching tools. Motivators in that you are progressing, while you are learning what aspects of training are most effective for you. Record keeping can include: the distance, the weather, the physical reactions such as breathing, sweat, and muscle soreness.

4. *The Shoe:* The feet are truly a critical component of distance walking and running. Immediately seek out a professional running shoe expert to measure your feet and determine if your foot strike is neutral, or needs stability due to a slight flair outside or inside; frequently called overpronation.

5. *A Realistic Distance Program*: A distance program involving impact requires gradual physical adaptation, muscular strength, and agility. Each of those components must be considered to keep injuries at bay and to avoid discouragement of the "too much, too soon" syndrome.

6. *Get Started*: There will never be a perfect time to begin a fitness program; life seems to always get in the way somehow. It is time to find what fitness level you are at now and begin.

Week 3
First Step, First Shoe

It is time to purchase your first "running" shoe. Walking shoes do not provide the flexibility of running shoes so it is best to begin with a running shoe. Running shoes give both the structured cushion needed for fast walking plus the stability which keeps the foot strike fairly balanced. Let's take a look at the aspects of choosing the correct shoe for your foot strike.

* *Check out your arch.* A high arch simply means you have it all going on the forefoot and heel; but little in between. A normal arch reveals all three parts of the foot will be used: the forefoot, the middle, and the heel. A flat foot has little if any arch.

* *Match your arch with a shoe which can provide the most normal gait.* Below are *three types of arches* which dictate the type of running shoe to be worn.

Under pronators, those with *high arches* are going to roll outward or supinate upon their landing. Continued outward rolling will create illotibial band pain, knee pain, lower limb pain, and possible hip problems. It is time to get a stability shoe which subtracts the outward roll. A built in stability bar with medium cushioning should help stabilize the foot strike.

Generally speaking those with *normal arches* will have a neutral or a more balanced foot strike. A normal arch suggests both forefoot and heel strike hit the ground fairly evenly thus allowing you to choose from many "neutral" running shoes. Neutral shoe wearers can also enjoy additional cushion and less built in stability. A neutral foot strike has a tendency to have less biomechanical challenges as well.

Those with *flat feet have little if any arch.* The tendency is to *overpronate* in two directions in order to gain foot strike stability. One direction is toward the outside of the heel first then the foot continues to rolls outward as the foot progresses to the toe off. Once again, an overpronator needs the correction of both stability and impact cushion. A severe overpronator may need more correction found in a motion control running shoe or in a custom made orthotic.

Week 4
The Core and More

Proper weight training for distance walking and running includes a series of progressive resistance exercises. Each exercise is specific to attain proper form, strength, and endurance. The exercises described below are known as *specificity of movement* exercises which increase overall leg and arm power, plus abdominal strength. These core exercises will improve overall posture and will prevent leaning forward as the body fatigues.

Your Turn:

Each exercise will build strength and power in both arms and legs. Begin 3 times per week for one month, progress to 4 times per week with a slight progression of weights added as directed. (See appendix #3 for illustrations.)

Step ups: Using 2 step stools of varying heights, step up with your right foot up on the stool then down, landing in both cases, flat footed. Do the entire motion quickly to simulate the walking and running movement. Work up to 25 repeats on each leg. Challenge of exercise is in the height and weight put onto the ankle. Begin with a 7-inch stool then go up to 11 inch or higher as your legs become stronger.
Effect: The repetitive quick up and down leg motion brings about faster leg turnover and adds to overall leg power.

Robot walk: Stand with your feet shoulder width apart with 1-2 lb. weights in each hand. Step forward with your right leg so that your foot is in the heel-strike position, and freeze. Then bring your right foot back to the starting position. Then step backwards with your right foot so that you are in the toe-off position, and again return your right foot to the starting position. Repeat 10 times and switch legs.
Effect: The practice of walking correctly with weights will strengthen both arms and legs and increase coordination of the walking movement.

Arm lunges: Place your feet in a small stride stance. Bend your arms and cup your hands around a one lb. weight in each hand. Mimic the back and forth flow of swinging your arms as you would while running, keeping your arms swinging close to each respective side part of the body. Vary the weights up to 5 lbs. Repeat both right and left arm swings 25 times. Challenge of this exercise will be the height of the arms while swinging and the weight held in each hand.
Effect: Increased efficiency of arms moving forward will keep the body propelled forward. Adding weight resistance will strengthen the arms and help increase efficiency of the arms moving forward.

Step up with arm swings: Combine the step up action with the arm swing such that the movement of fast walking or running is done. Repeat 25 times.

Effect: Leg and arm efficiency and strength will help the body attain walking and running coordination, strength, and power.

Bicep curls: Stand with knees slightly bent, holding a 5 to 10 lb. dumbbell in each hand. Curl weights to shoulders with the palms facing you. Pause, than slowly lower to start. Do 3 sets of 10 repetitions.

Effect: Bicep strength will help overall arm power and give a "lift" to the foot strike as you move forward while walking or running. This reduces the plodding effect one sees with many runners.

Core circling: Stand up with feet hip length apart, moving both arms sideward to the left as far as they can go, while rotating the core in the same direction Repeat to the right. Keep hands in a loose fist. Keep your feet in place. Repeat 10 times.

Effect: The movement of the hip flexors and trunk area will add flexibility to your torso, plus strengthen your shoulders and arms

Waist twists: Stand with feet hip length apart holding a 5-10 lb. medicine ball with both hands at lower chest level. Gently twist left with an exaggerated left shoulder movement continuing the twist until your waist, shoulders, neck, and head turn about 90 degrees, or so you can see behind you. Slowly repeat the twist in the same manner, but toward the right. Aim for 25 alternating sides.

Effect: Exaggerated waist twists give forward momentum to the walker and runner by developing the entire shoulder, deltoid, latissimus dorsal, and upper back muscles. Twists help strengthen the upper body plus will add flexibility to both waist and core muscles.

Pectoral chest openers: Place your feet hip length apart with arms raised sideward, both bent in at the elbows at shoulder height, palms cupped and facing inward. Slowly and steadily bring both bent arms back as far as possible so as to form a V in the scapular of your back. Repeat 10 times. Challenge will be if 3lb to 5lb. weights are added.

Effect: Openers add strength in the shoulders and arm muscle groups plus the core while increasing balance and posture while standing, walking, or running.

Chest presses: Place the feet hip length apart with arms bent at elbow chest level; with a slight arch in the back bring both bent arms back so each arm is parallel to the side of the body. Do 3 sets of 25, with 1-2 lb. weights.

Effect: This brief range of chest movement will increase shoulder and chest muscle strength while developing core muscles.

French curls: Hold a 5 to 7 pound dumbbell overhead in each hand. Bend elbows and allow hands to lower behind the head until the lower arms are parallel to the floor. Return to start. Do 3 sets of 10. End this strengthening exercise with a mountain pose.

Effect: The triceps will be strengthened as will total arm strength. The stretching will help your posture and your core. The form and range of motion is more important than the amount of weight lifted.

Core and More Exercises
(See appendix 3 & 4 for illustrations)

Type of Exercise	Frequency Sets=work up to	Effect	Weight Intensity
Plyometric Step-ups	Every other day 3 sets 25	Increases leg turnover and power	1-2 lb. wt.
Plyometric Robot Walk	Every other day 10 times each leg	Increases leg turnover and power	1 lb. wt.
Plyometric Rocket	Every other day 30 times each leg	Increases leg turnover and power	1-2 lb. wt.
Plyometric 1-leg march	Every other day 10 times each leg	Increases leg turnover and power	1-3 lb. wt.
Plyometric Arm side lunges	Every other day 3 sets of 25	Strong arms propel body forward	1-5 lb. wt.
Plyometric Step up w/ arm lunge	Every other day 3 sets of 25	Increases leg and arm efficiency & strength	1-5 lb. wt.-arms, 1-2 lb. wt.-legs
Plyometric Arm swings	5 days 25 times	Increase flexibility to torso and hip flexors	1 lb. wt.
Plyometric Pectoral chest openers	5 days 3 sets of 25	Increase shoulder, arm, and core strength while opening up chest muscles	1-5 lb. wt.
Plyometric Core circling	5 days 4 x left & right	Movement of hip flexors increases flexibility and range of motion	No weight
Plyometric Toe raises	5 days 10 x in 3 directions	Increase ankle strength while increasing flexibility for quick toe off	No weight
Strength Training 3-dimensional abdominal curls	5 days 2 sets of 25 in each direction	Strong abs & oblique's stabilize the pelvis, strengthens core resulting in better posture	None-10 lbs. wt.
Strength Training Plank	5 days 3 times	Increase strength in abs and back muscles will improve forward movement coordination	None
Strength Training French Curls	5 days 3 sets of 10	Increase triceps strength for total arm strength and total arm stretch	5-10 lb. wt.
Strength Training Chest Presses	5 days 25 times	Increase shoulder and chest muscle strength while developing the core muscles	1-5 lb. wt.
Strength Training Bicep Curls	5 days 3 sets of 10	Bicep strength will increase overall arm power as you move forward	5-10 lb. wt.
Strength Training Back extensions	5 days 25 times	Lower back and hips will become stretched & strengthened; posture will be improved	0-10 lb. wt.

You must learn to walk before you can run. Lynn Gray

<u>**Week Beginning**</u>   /   /

Daily Schedule – Week 1

Miscellaneous Comments

Date	Monday		○ _____
_____	_____		○ _____
Distance	_____		○ _____
Intensity	_____		○ _____
Cross-	_____		○ _____
Train	_____		
Weather	_____		
Date	Tuesday		○ _____
_____	_____		○ _____
Distance	_____		○ _____
Intensity	_____		○ _____
Cross-	_____		○ _____
Train	_____		
Weather	_____		
Date	Wednesday		○ _____
_____	_____		○ _____
Distance	_____		○ _____
Intensity	_____		○ _____
Cross-	_____		○ _____
Train	_____		
Weather	_____		
Date	Thursday		○ _____
_____	_____		○ _____
Distance	_____		○ _____
Intensity	_____		○ _____
Cross-	_____		○ _____
Train	_____		
Weather	_____		
Date	Friday		○ _____
_____	_____		○ _____
Distance	_____		○ _____
Intensity	_____		○ _____
Cross-	_____		○ _____
Train	_____		
Weather	_____		
Date	Saturday		○ _____
_____	_____		○ _____
Distance	_____		○ _____
Intensity	_____		○ _____
Cross-	_____		○ _____
Train	_____		
Weather	_____		
Date	Sunday		○ _____
_____	_____		○ _____
Distance	_____		○ _____
Intensity	_____		○ _____
Cross-	_____		○ _____
Train	_____		
Weather	_____		

"The body never lies." Martha Graham

<u>Week Beginning</u>   /   /

Daily Schedule – Week 2

Miscellaneous Comment

Date	Monday		○	_____
			○	_____
_____	_____		○	_____
Distance	_____		○	_____
Intensity	_____		○	_____
Cross-	_____			
Train	_____			
Weather	_____			
Date	Tuesday		○	_____
			○	_____
_____	_____		○	_____
Distance	_____		○	_____
Intensity	_____		○	_____
Cross-	_____			
Train	_____			
Weather	_____			
Date	Wednesday		○	_____
			○	_____
_____	_____		○	_____
Distance	_____		○	_____
Intensity	_____		○	_____
Cross-	_____			
Train	_____			
Weather	_____			
Date	Thursday		○	_____
			○	_____
_____	_____		○	_____
Distance	_____		○	_____
Intensity	_____		○	_____
Cross-	_____			
Train	_____			
Weather	_____			
Date	Friday		○	_____
			○	_____
_____	_____		○	_____
Distance	_____		○	_____
Intensity	_____		○	_____
Cross-	_____			
Train	_____			
Weather	_____			
Date	Saturday		○	_____
			○	_____
_____	_____		○	_____
Distance	_____		○	_____
Intensity	_____		○	_____
Cross-	_____			
Train	_____			
Weather	_____			
Date	Sunday		○	_____
			○	_____
_____	_____		○	_____
Distance	_____		○	_____
Intensity	_____		○	_____
Cross-	_____			
Train	_____			
Weather	_____			

"After dinner, rest a while, after supper walk a mile." Arabic proverb

Week Beginning   /   /
Daily Schedule – Week 3
Miscellaneous Comments

Date	Monday		
Distance		○	_____
Intensity		○	_____
Cross-Train		○	_____
Weather		○	_____
		○	_____

Date	Tuesday		
Distance		○	_____
Intensity		○	_____
Cross-Train		○	_____
Weather		○	_____
		○	_____

Date	Wednesday		
Distance		○	_____
Intensity		○	_____
Cross-Train		○	_____
Weather		○	_____
		○	_____

Date	Thursday		
Distance		○	_____
Intensity		○	_____
Cross-Train		○	_____
Weather		○	_____
		○	_____

Date	Friday		
Distance		○	_____
Intensity		○	_____
Cross-Train		○	_____
Weather		○	_____
		○	_____

Date	Saturday		
Distance		○	_____
Intensity		○	_____
Cross-Train		○	_____
Weather		○	_____
		○	_____

Date	Sunday		
Distance		○	_____
Intensity		○	_____
Cross-Train		○	_____
Weather		○	_____
		○	_____

"The physically fit can enjoy their vices." Lloyd Percival

<u>**Week Beginning**</u>   **/**   **/**
Daily Schedule – Week 4
Miscellaneous Comments

Date	Monday		
		○	_____
		○	_____
Distance		○	_____
Intensity		○	_____
Cross-		○	_____
Train			
Weather			
Date	Tuesday		
		○	_____
		○	_____
Distance		○	_____
Intensity		○	_____
Cross-		○	_____
Train			
Weather			
Date	Wednesday		
		○	_____
		○	_____
Distance		○	_____
Intensity		○	_____
Cross-		○	_____
Train			
Weather			
Date	Thursday		
		○	_____
		○	_____
Distance		○	_____
Intensity		○	_____
Cross-		○	_____
Train			
Weather			
Date	Friday		
		○	_____
		○	_____
Distance		○	_____
Intensity		○	_____
Cross-		○	_____
Train			
Weather			
Date	Saturday		
		○	_____
		○	_____
Distance		○	_____
Intensity		○	_____
Cross-		○	_____
Train			
Weather			
Date	Sunday		
		○	_____
		○	_____
Distance		○	_____
Intensity		○	_____
Cross-		○	_____
Train			
Weather			

Workout Weeks 5-8
Becoming a Cardio-Walker

Pick the level you are currently at. Follow this beginner schedule at that current level so there is a gradual adaptation of impact on the body.

Weeks 5-6: *note first number is cardio walk, 2nd number is easy walk with arms on the sides...see Week 6 for complete guide on how to cardio walk

Level	Intensity	Frequency	Distance	Time	Weeks
Beginner	cardio walk *2 to 1	4 days	1-3 miles	35 min	5-6
CORE & MORE Stretching		2 days 4 days			
Int. Beg	cardio walk *4 to 1	4 days	3-4 miles	60 min	5-6
CORE & MORE Stretching		2 days 4 days			
Adv Beg	cardio walk *5 to 1	5 days	4 + miles	1.5 hrs.	5-6
CORE & MORE Stretching		2 days 4 days			

Weeks 7-8: use *1.5 lb. heavy hands while cardio walking

Level	Intensity	Frequency	Distance	Time	Weeks
Beginner	cardio walk *2 to 1	4 days	1-3 miles	35 min	7-8
CORE & MORE Stretching		2 days 4 days			
Int. Beg	cardio walk *4 to 1	4 days	3-4 miles	60 min	7-8
CORE & MORE Stretching		2 days 4 days			
Adv Beg	cardio walk *5 to 1	5 days	4 + miles	1.5 hrs.	7-8
CORE & MORE Stretching		2 days 4 days			

Cardio Walking terms
* Intensity = speed and form of walk
* Frequency = number of days per week
* Basic Stretches and Weight Training - Refer to the illustrations in appendix
* Record your weekly progress in the journal

Week 5
Cardio Walking Brings Youthful Results

It is a fact that the most common and simple form of aerobic exercise is walking. Walking can indeed subtract middle age ailments for us baby boomers. One term for steady, vigorous walking is athletically called "cardio walking." Many people turn to cardio walking as an alternative to running due to worn out cartilage in their knees, hip, or back problems. Also, some of us would rather briskly walk because the faster motion does increase the metabolic rate.

So why is the pursuing of cardio walking an exercise of interest for us middle age folks entering our prime of life? It is during the thirties, forties, and fifties, that we face the biggest stresses in our lives. These are the primary parenting years, a time when we have work-related stress due to added career responsibilities, plus many of us have ailing parents who need care during this time. Increased stress creates sleep problems as well, putting us into our beds with multiple thoughts and concerns not resolved. Plus, too many things on our minds challenge our mental clarity and can make us more absent minded. On top of these mental stress realities, we get to see the aging process revealing itself as well. Men and women in their forties and fifties experience weight gain and see additional flab due to a slower metabolism. At the same time men notice a loss or thinning of hair, and women are beginning to notice more wrinkles. All of these physical realities motivate baby boomers to seek out a fitness plan which will help them feel and look better.

Cardio walking is a good way to relieve the stresses of a job by having time away from your work and family to reflect on problems allowing creative energies to surface. Walking gives one time to work out many worries so they are not carried through the evening when relaxation and sleep should occur. Increased circulation of oxygen and blood increases our response time and memory. Taking a brisk walk for an hour of two will induce physical fatigue and help promote a deeper sleep.

Cardio walking also exercises the arms and legs evenly. The arms and legs become toned and strengthened. Flexibility is increased in the joints, connective muscles and bones. Since walking is a low-impact exercise it does not place stress on the bones of the spine, which prevents back problems and enables those with knee problems to exercise without getting knee pain.

Brisk walking increases circulation which in turn nourishes the collagen fibers, making them more elastic which helps the skin remain firm and smooth. Since walking builds muscles under the skin, wrinkles will smooth out slightly, giving us a more youthful appearance.

Fast pace walking is an effective weight-loss exercise. As we age our metabolism slows down. Our body fat increases as muscle decreases and extra weight on women soon appears on the hips, thighs, and abdomen. Men gain body fat on their abdomen and chest. Walking at a faster but comfortable pace will tone muscle in the thighs, buttocks, and abdomen so the body will look less flabby and more toned.

As we age, our digestive system loses speed thus making the food we eat take longer to move through our system. This slow down leads to stomach cramps, gas, constipation, and can develop into colon cancer during our late forties and on. A steady brisk walking program *will speed up the entire digestive* system so that food moves through more efficiently.

Speed or power walking is also referred to as "cardio walking" because it strengthens your cardiovascular system. By age 45 your maximum oxygen has decreased by almost 20 percent, meaning that the body takes in and delivers to the muscles 20 percent less oxygen. Brisk walking can prevent some of this loss by increasing the efficiency with which the muscle cells take oxygen from the blood. Fast movement subtracts the amount of shrinkage of lung tissues and increases the development of chest muscles which helps both inhalation and exhalation. Since our arteries become less flexible as we age and become clogged with cholesterol, the narrowing of arteries occurs which then slows down blood flow to the heart. Cardio walking helps to open up the arteries and flush out the cholesterol or at the very least prevent further buildup. This opening up of arteries will also aid in lowering high blood pressure. Women who complain about the onset of varicose veins can be relieved to know walking increases circulation in the legs and helps prevent or minimize unsightly veins.

Most of us "baby boomers" will face many challenges and changes in our lives as the aging process begins. Cardio walking can help lessen and prevent mid-life health problems. Brisk walking will promote weight loss, reduce blood pressure, relieve stress, and add tone to your body. Establishing a vigorous walking program will help one look and feel younger, making the journey through the prime of life and the years after, a more enjoyable and healthy process.

Week 6
The Cardio Walk

Like any other sport, the better form you engage in while performing the more efficient and faster the body will move. Proper form in cardio walking will allow the body mechanics to accept it for long periods of time. Good technique and posture result in the gradual development of an efficient walk and future running movement.

Let's check out how you currently walk. Have a family member or friend do a brief video of you while walking down the block. Are the shoulders slightly hunched over? That could manifest later into a sore back and tight calves. Do the shoulders appear stiff? That would indicate a certain amount of stress you are under causing the shoulders to not relax. You need to put the shoulders down and arch the back a bit. Does it look like you walk like a robot, with a stiff torso, neck, shoulders, and legs? Eventually, that will tire you out physically and mentally and not facilitate a relaxing walk. Finally, take a look at your arms. Are they hanging by your sides like weights and barely moving while walking? The arms should be moving in unison while walking, pushing forward at a 90 degree angle for forward momentum.

Time to Practice

Each technique should be practiced at least for ½ mile or 5 minutes.

Practice # 1 – Posture: Tuck the chin in, holding your head in a neutral position without looking down or up. Visualize having a string running along your spine and out of the top of your head in a straight line. Arch the back slightly while moving forward.

Practice #2 – Breathing: Inhalation and exhalation should be even; allowing for more rapid breaths as the pace quickens. Consistent breathing will bring oxygen to the cells bringing more energy into your body. Practice relaxed breathing being careful to not hyperventilate. Become aware of what your breathing rhythms are at different speeds: slow pace, medium pace, and fast pace.

Practice #3 – Foot movement: Your gait should come to you naturally; do not over stride or under stride. Avoid making your stride too narrow since hip problems can result. The forward motion of each foot lines up to the hip to shoulder and the foot placement is straight ahead, not pigeon footed, or facing inward.

Practice #4 – Arms: The arms should be held at a 90 degree angle. Pump your arms straight forward and back, being certain to brush the sides of your hips to check. Put a safety pin just above your hip, making sure your arm brushes over it each time it moves forward. Practice this arm pump in front of a mirror with 1-3 pound hand held weights. Remember to keep a slight arch in your back so distance walking does not hurt your back nor put too much weight on the shins and knees. Vigorous moving arms result in a stronger upper body and result in a more balanced forward movement.

Practice #5 – Shoulders: Your shoulders should be held square, being careful not to hunch them inward; again keep a slight arch in the back.

Practice #6 – Foot Strike: Proper stepping should include a hip to shoulder-wide stance. Your heel strikes first and then move from heel to toe to get the "toe off" momentum. Wearing a cushioned, stability running shoe of medium weight will help accommodate this swift heel to toe movement. Keep your knees relaxed with a slight bend.

Practice #7 – Hip Movement: Synchronize arm and hip movement. Allow your hips to rotate downward and forward as your leg reaches forward. This gives the muscles and joints in your arms and legs a total workout.

Practice # 8 – Before and After the Cardio Walk Workout:

    A. Warm up slowly ½ mile by gradually getting "in cardio walking position"
    B. Stop and stretch the hamstrings, calves, quadriceps (see stretches in appendix)
    C. Remember to hydrate each twenty minutes or so. Wear a water belt if water is not readily available.
    D. Warm-down ½ mile, relax your entire form with easy walking
    E. When finished, pour ice water on the legs. This will prevent any muscular inflammation and will help to prevent common starting injuries such as shin splints.

Week 7
Staying Uninjured Along the Way

Cardio walking is considerably a low-impact form of exercise which lessens chances of injuries. One foot is always on the ground and reduces the full force of the entire body hitting the ground at once. However when you factor in duration, the time on your feet together with a hard walking surface, overuse injuries can occur. To prevent overuse injuries to the muscles, tendons and ligaments begin to assess your current walking resources: the shoe, your form and technique.

Cardio walking necessitates a running shoe with flexibility and stability. The flexibility is necessary so the heel to toe movement flows naturally in one rolling movement consistent to the anatomy of the foot and ankle. Cardio walkers and runners do not want stiffness, tightness, or a feeling of restriction with the running shoe since those factors will hamper a natural gait. Wearing a flexible running shoe will also help accommodate a swift heel to toe movement. The avid cardio walker or runner should work on strengthening the ankles with toe raises, so as to avoid an improper foot strike caused by weak ankles allowing the angle of the foot to land outward or inward.

In most impact sports proper form and technique are critical components for the body's biomechanical adaptation. Let's review the basics of cardio walking form. The shoulders should be held square, being careful not to hunch forward. Remember to keep the pelvis in to prevent a slight forward bend. The heel to toe movement has a continual flow with the feet aimed straight so excessive angling left or right does not occur. The stride allows for a slight bend of the knee and the stride span should be about 12" to 16".

There are other factors which keep us moving forward without injury. Here are tried and true practices each cardio walker or runner should integrate into their fitness routine. It is the prevention of injuries that allows us to stay in the game and progress week after week.

- At least once a week do your workouts on *soft ground*-treadmills do count. Try to avoid concrete whenever possible.

- Check your running surface…make sure you *change sides* of the road if it has "slopes."

- Use a 4 foot long *foam roller* to smooth out tight muscles. The weight of your body goes on top of the roller and can be used for major muscle groups such as the iliotibial band, the calves, the quads, the back, etc. Foam rollers are available at most sports stores and they functions much like a rolling pin smoothing out dough. The "stick" is another tool to smooth out tight muscles and serves to keep muscles both fluid and agile.

- *Weight train* major leg, core, and arm muscle groups with light hand weights and high repetitions. Light weights are important and allow for an increase of range of motion.

High repetitions will increase muscular strength. Muscles which are strong and of equal length tend to protect overuse injuries in specific spots such as the Achilles or hamstrings.

- Practice *yoga or a flexibility class* once a week, then choose 2-3 moves from the class and practice each day. Muscle tightness results in poor posture, contributing to unequal distribution of weight on your legs, core, and upper body. Stretches must be held 15 seconds and should be static vs. ballistic to avoid overstretching or tearing muscles.

- Apply *cold water* to your leg muscles following each cardio walking or running workout.

- Train up *gradually;* add only 10% of your mileage each week. If you are walking or running 10 miles per week, the next week goes up to 11 miles. The mind will want more, but the body will eventually refuse with a remark called "overuse injury."

- *Hydrate* before, during, and after the run. Hydration allows the muscles to stay warm and the joints to move more fluidly.

- Keep your running shoes fresh and *rotate* every other day. Check for worn out areas which reveal an uneven foot strike. Many injuries occur due to the resulting foot strike from the running shoe which puts the body out of natural alignment. Being fitted professionally goes a long way in preventing foot strike injuries. Long distance cardio walkers and runners are advised to get a heavier cushioned/stability running shoe.

- Get a *gait analysis* to check out your running or walking form and gait. Most people have a part(s) of their body moving out of proper form alignment for efficient forward movement. This can be corrected by the running shoe and of course proper form and technique.

- If injuries are continual, consider getting an *insert or fitted for orthotics.* Remember, flexibility and strength exercises plus correct running shoes will resolve most injuries.

Week 8
Improving Range of Motion

All things in our life should be balanced, so why not our walking and running movement? The more muscle mass you develop, the tighter the muscles become which decreases range of motion. A decrease in range of motion forces you to rely on the same muscles, tendon and ligaments which become overused then eventually inflamed forcing you to take time off. Stretching keeps your muscle groups balanced so you can use them all. Stretching increases range of motion so the landing pattern becomes more evenly distributed. What are other benefits of increasing our flexibility?

Flexibility exercises contribute to muscular relaxation, range of motion within the joints, improved muscular balance, increased speed of movement and very importantly, performance. Most significantly, stretching or adding a flexibility program will reduce injuries. We are born with many factors which limit our ROM – range of motion mostly because of our joint structure itself. This factor, together with the muscular activity which running provides, will result in greater limits of our range of motion.

What are the major groups of flexibility exercises which will help develop range of motion?

Static stretching: holding a stretch for a period of time. Yoga and Tai Chi exemplify slow holding of a stretched muscle. Static flexibility exercises will lengthen and balance your major muscle groups while increasing the health of the synovial fluid in the joints. Increased coordination results from holding a position for a period of time, not to mention balance and strength. There is no better weight training one can do than to use their own body weight in various positions to strengthen strategic muscles as it relates to running or whatever sport one pursues.

Dynamic stretching: – waking up your slow twitch muscles and getting a quicker range of motion to improve and maintain both the speed and force of muscle contractions. For example, by lifting your leg up and down with little or no additional weight not only increases your range of motion, but allows body mechanics to be more coordinated and efficient. Flexibility exercises specific to the walking or running motion clearly will prepare the athlete with increased fluid motion and minimum resistance due to improved coordination.

Follow the series of stretches after a 5 minute warm-up of walking and repeat after your workout. Hold each position for 15-20 seconds. This series should take about 10 minutes. (See appendix #4 for illustrations.)

1. Plank: Lay face down with the body absolutely straight and place arms just under the shoulders and lift the body up with the strength of the arms, holding the legs up using the strength of the toes. Have the entire body as parallel to the ground as possible. Hold this position for 5-10 breaths.

Effect: Increases strength and flexibility in the deep back muscles, the glutes, and the hamstrings which improve posture and balance. The toe flexing helps with toeing off.

2. Spinal twist: Sit on the mat and bring the right knee across the body and toward the left hip, placing the foot next to the sit bone. Hold for 5-10 seconds, and then switch to the other side. This is also a very effective stretch for the hip flexors.
   Effect: Walking and running require a moderate whole body twist. This upper body twist helps balance the body but results in gait economy and increases range of motion of the stride.

3. Butterfly stretch: Sitting down with a straight upper-body, press your feet together. You can increase this groin stretch by bending straight down with your torso straight and simultaneously reach your hands in front of you.
   Effect: Abductors will have greater length making the forward stride more balanced. The groin muscles will stay loose so the hip and pelvic area do not become tight and stiff.

4. Quadriceps stretch: Using a fence, tree, or wall as support, reach back with the right hand and grasp the right foot and ankle, being careful that your hips are facing forward; repeat with the other leg.
   Effect: Tight quads force us to increase the use of knee impact and lower leg muscles such as the quads, plus the shin area. From the knee down leg strength is limited and more impact on our "weak links" results. Increase of quad strength helps us distribute impact of those larger muscle groups versus the knee and above.

5. Hamstring stretch with rope: Begin by lying on your back and looping a towel or rope around one foot. The other leg should be lying flat down. Using the towel or rope as the "puller," lift the leg up till you feel a slight pull, than contract the quadriceps, repeat with the other leg. This is a great stretch for women since hamstring pulls are very common.
   Effect: The stride width will increase giving an increased foot strike landing distance. A full stride aids economy of movement and can decrease the perceived exertion level quite a bit.

6. Calf stretch: Use a fence, tree, or wall for support place one foot behind the other. With the front knee slightly bent, back knee straight, and heel down, lean hips forward. Feel the pull in your calf muscle and hold. Repeat on the opposite side. The calf stretch can help prevent tight Achilles plus will reduce the onset of shin splints, a malady which affects beginner walkers and runners especially.
   Effect: Tight calves are the most common malady with both women and men. Women many times wear heels and men have larger muscle groups surrounding the Achilles. A stretched calf muscle reduces the pull on the Achilles tendon and the ligaments and tendons from the heel up. In addition, loose calves reduce the work on the shins which go a long way to preventing shin splints.

7. Toe raises: Place feet less than hip width apart. Rock slowly up on the balls of the feet as high as possible as slowly back down onto the heels. Next splay the feet outward and do the same up and down motion. Finally, place feet inward, pigeon toed, and repeat the same up and down motion. Repeat 8-10 repetitions in each direction.
   Effect: The ankles will become stronger and more flexible. The toe off movement while walking and running will become more natural.

8. Abdominal curls: Lying on the back with knees bent and feet on the floor with hands lying on top of the thighs, raise the torso up and slightly forward with the forward movement of the arms, then return slowly downward. Be careful to lead with the chin to avoid stressing the neck. For the oblique, repeat the same slow raised motion, but gently twist right part of the body so the right elbow heads toward the left knee. Alternate this movement on the other side; left *elbow to right knee. Begin 10 repetitions in each direction, then work up* to 25. A challenge would be to have a light weight in your hands while moving forward and to the sides.
   Effect: The abdominals become strong enough to stabilize the pelvis giving the "core" a stronger center resulting in better posture and a more stable landing strike while running or walking.

9. Core circling: Stand with feet hip length apart, hands on hips. Bend slightly and circle the torso clockwise 4 times, then reverse 4 times.
   Effect: The stretching movement of the hip flexors increases flexibility and allows an increased range of motion.

10. Sit down hip flexor stretch: Sit down on a chair and cross the right leg over the left knee, having the right ankle resting on the right knee. Gently bend forward at the waist allowing the arms to reach downward to the floor. As muscular tension is felt in the right hip, gently rock left and right to obtain an increased stretch. Repeat this same procedure with the left leg crossed over right knee.
    Effect: Increasing flexibility with the hip flexors reduces the propensity for impact on the IT Band (iliotibial band); a major source of injuries for walkers and runners alike. The distribution of impact on the sides of the leg above the knee is reduced due to increased flexibility in the glute and hip area.

11. Wedge calf stretch: Place both feet hip length apart on a gradual raised slant platform such as a plywood or yoga wedge. Stand up on the wedge and push forward and downward with the arms until they near the ground. Hold for 15 seconds. Return to normal stance, and repeat same movement with feet splayed outward, then with feet facing inward.
    Effect: This 3-dimensional stretch will increase length of calf and hamstring muscles, which will reduce tightness in the Achilles area and lessen chances of shin splints for both walkers and runners.

"There are risks and costs to a program of action. But they are far less than the long-range risks of comfortable inaction." John F. Kennedy

Week Beginning _____ / _____ / _____
Daily Schedule – Week 5
Miscellaneous Comments

Date	Monday		
		○	_____
	_____	○	_____
Distance	_____	○	_____
Intensity	_____	○	_____
Cross-	_____	○	_____
Train	_____		
Weather	_____		

Date	Tuesday		
		○	_____
	_____	○	_____
Distance	_____	○	_____
Intensity	_____	○	_____
Cross-	_____	○	_____
Train	_____		
Weather	_____		

Date	Wednesday		
		○	_____
	_____	○	_____
Distance	_____	○	_____
Intensity	_____	○	_____
Cross-	_____	○	_____
Train	_____		
Weather	_____		

Date	Thursday		
		○	_____
	_____	○	_____
Distance	_____	○	_____
Intensity	_____	○	_____
Cross-	_____	○	_____
Train	_____		
Weather	_____		

Date	Friday		
		○	_____
	_____	○	_____
Distance	_____	○	_____
Intensity	_____	○	_____
Cross-	_____	○	_____
Train	_____		
Weather	_____		

Date	Saturday		
		○	_____
	_____	○	_____
Distance	_____	○	_____
Intensity	_____	○	_____
Cross-	_____	○	_____
Train	_____		
Weather	_____		

Date	Sunday		
		○	_____
	_____	○	_____
Distance	_____	○	_____
Intensity	_____	○	_____
Cross-	_____	○	_____
Train	_____		
Weather	_____		

"Nature, time and patience are the three great physicians." Proverb

Week Beginning   /   /
Daily Schedule – Week 6
Miscellaneous Comments

Date	Monday				
_____			○	_____
Distance			○	_____
Intensity			○	_____
Cross-			○	_____
Train			○	_____
Weather				
Date	**Tuesday**		○	_____
_____			○	_____
Distance			○	_____
Intensity			○	_____
Cross-			○	_____
Train				
Weather				
Date	**Wednesday**		○	_____
_____			○	_____
Distance			○	_____
Intensity			○	_____
Cross-			○	_____
Train				
Weather				
Date	**Thursday**		○	_____
_____			○	_____
Distance			○	_____
Intensity			○	_____
Cross-			○	_____
Train				
Weather				
Date	**Friday**		○	_____
_____			○	_____
Distance			○	_____
Intensity			○	_____
Cross-			○	_____
Train				
Weather				
Date	**Saturday**		○	_____
_____			○	_____
Distance			○	_____
Intensity			○	_____
Cross-			○	_____
Train				
Weather				
Date	**Sunday**		○	_____
_____			○	_____
Distance			○	_____
Intensity			○	_____
Cross-			○	_____
Train				
Weather				

"Strength is a matter of the made-up mind." John Beecher

<u>Week Beginning</u>   /   /

Daily Schedule – Week 7

Miscellaneous Comments

Date	Monday		
Distance		○	_____
Intensity		○	_____
Cross-Train		○	_____
Weather		○	_____
		○	_____

Date	Tuesday		
Distance		○	_____
Intensity		○	_____
Cross-Train		○	_____
Weather		○	_____
		○	_____

Date	Wednesday		
Distance		○	_____
Intensity		○	_____
Cross-Train		○	_____
Weather		○	_____
		○	_____

Date	Thursday		
Distance		○	_____
Intensity		○	_____
Cross-Train		○	_____
Weather		○	_____
		○	_____

Date	Friday		
Distance		○	_____
Intensity		○	_____
Cross-Train		○	_____
Weather		○	_____
		○	_____

Date	Saturday		
Distance		○	_____
Intensity		○	_____
Cross-Train		○	_____
Weather		○	_____
		○	_____

Date	Sunday		
Distance		○	_____
Intensity		○	_____
Cross-Train		○	_____
Weather		○	_____
		○	_____

"Outside movement, increases inward thought." Lynn Gray

Week Beginning ____/____/____
Daily Schedule – Week 8
Miscellaneous Comments

Date	Monday		
Distance Intensity Cross-Train Weather		○ ○ ○ ○ ○	_____ _____ _____ _____ _____
Date	Tuesday		
Distance Intensity Cross-Train Weather		○ ○ ○ ○ ○	_____ _____ _____ _____ _____
Date	Wednesday		
Distance Intensity Cross-Train Weather		○ ○ ○ ○ ○	_____ _____ _____ _____ _____
Date	Thursday		
Distance Intensity Cross-Train Weather		○ ○ ○ ○ ○	_____ _____ _____ _____ _____
Date	Friday		
Distance Intensity Cross-Train Weather		○ ○ ○ ○ ○	_____ _____ _____ _____ _____
Date	Saturday		
Distance Intensity Cross-Train Weather		○ ○ ○ ○ ○	_____ _____ _____ _____ _____
Date	Sunday		
Distance Intensity Cross-Train Weather		○ ○ ○ ○ ○	_____ _____ _____ _____ _____

Phase 2
Walk to Jog

Ratio Training

Weeks 9 - 16

Workout Weeks 9-16
Cardio Walking to Easy Running

Notes: Pick the level you are currently at. Follow this schedule at that current level so there is a gradual adaptation of impact on the body.

Weeks 9 – 10: c/w = cardio walk, x = @ of sets to repeat, jog = easy effort

Levels	Monday	Tuesday	Wednesday	Thursday	Friday	Saturday	Sunday
Beginner: 1st #= walk 2nd #= c/w	Conditioning exercises	Go 20 min. in one direction; turn around and go 19 min. or less- c/w	Go 20 min. in one direction; turn around and go 19 min. or less	3/8 x 3	Rest/wts	3/8 x 3	Go 20 min. in one direction; turn around and go 19 min. or less
Intermediate- cardio walk to jog 1st # = c/w 2nd # = jog	Conditioning exercises	25 min. non-stop cardio walk/jog comb.; turn around and go same distance faster	25 min. non-stop cardio walk/jog comb.; turn around and go same distance faster	2/10 x 3	Rest/wts	2/10 x 3	25 min. non-stop cardio walk/jog comb.; turn around and go same distance faster
Advanced- jog to run 1st# = jog 2nd # = run	Conditioning exercises	30 min. non-stop jog; return in 29 min or less	30 min. non-stop jog; return in 29 min or less	15 min. non-stop jog, 2/4 x 2	Rest/wts	15 min. non-stop jog, 2/4 x 2	30 min. non-stop jog; return in 29 min or less

Weeks 11-12: High Stepping=exaggerated leg lift while walking
**   Bounding = while in running motion**

Levels	Monday	Tuesday	Wednesday	Thursday	Friday	Saturday	Sunday
Beginner	rest	Set: 3 min c/w, 1 min. high stepping 3 min. easy walk x 4 sets	Set: 3 min c/w, 1 min. high stepping , 3 min. easy walk x 6 sets	3/8 x 3	Rest/wts	w/o	Set: 3 min c/w, 1 min. high stepping , 3 min. easy walk x 6-7 sets
Intermediate- walk to jog	rest	Set: 3 min jog, 1 min walking high step, 2 min walk X 8	Set: 3 min jog, 1 min walking high step, 2 min walk X 8-9 sets	2/10 x 3	Rest/wts	w/o	Set: 3 min jog, 1 min walking high step, 2 min walk X 10 sets
Advanced- jog to run	rest	Set: 3 min run, 1 min bounding, 2 min jog x 6-7 sets	Set: 3 min run, 1 min bounding, 2 min jog x 6-7 sets	Set: 5/2- 5 min. jog, 2 min run x 4-5 sets	Rest/wts	w/o	Set: 3 min run, 1 min bounding, 2 min jog x 7-8 sets

Weeks 13 – 15:

Levels	Monday	Tuesday	Wednesday	Thursday	Friday	Saturday	Sunday
Beginner	w/o	Set: 3 min c/w, 3 min. easy walk x 5 sets	Repeat workout above	3/8 x 5	Rest/wts	Repeat workout above	Set: 3 min c/w, 3 min. easy walk x 7 sets
Intermediate- walk to run	w/o	Set: 3 min jog, 2 min walk X 8 sets	Repeat workout above	2/10 x 3	Rest/wts	Repeat workout above	Set: 3 min jog, 2 min walk X 10 sets
Advanced- jog-run	w/o	Set: 3 min run, 2 min. jog x 7 sets	Repeat workout above	Set: 5/2- 5 min. jog, 2 min run x 7 sets	Rest/wts	Repeat workout above	Set: 3 min run, 2 min jog x 10 sets

Week 16:
Striders = Divide 1 minute into three parts: easy effort, medium effort, fast effort

Levels	Monday	Tuesday	Wednesday	Thursday	Friday	Saturday	Sunday
Beginner	rest	Go 20 min. in one direction; turn around and go faster; 2 x 100 yd striders	Go 20 min. in one direction; turn around and go 19 min. or less; 2 x 100 yd. striders	3/8 x 3	Rest/wts	3/8 x 3; 2 x 100 yd. striders	5K event
Intermedi ate-cardio walk to jog	rest	25 min. non-stop cardio walk/jog comb.; turn around & go faster; 3 striders	25 min. non-stop cardio walk/jog comb.; turn around and go same distance faster; 3 striders	2/10 x 3	Rest/wts	2/10 x 3; 3 striders	5K event
Advanced- jog to run	rest	30 min. non-stop jog; return in 29 min or less	30 min. non-stop jog; return in 29 min or less	15 min. non-stop jog, 2/4 x 2	Rest/wts	15 min. non-stop jog, 2/4 x 2	5K event

Week 9
Cardio Walking to Jogging

The switch from brisk walking to easy running begins when we leave the comfort and balance of having one foot on the ground versus just having one striking at a time. The body by now should be strong enough to handle the impact. Leg and arm strength are developed to a point where the arms move forward as if "pulling a rope" and the legs move the same speed as the arms move. Biomechanically the body should be ready for the alternating foot strikes. However, let's do a bit of confidence work before the first launch.

- *Check your balance.* Place two feet together, lift one leg up to the mid-shin and hold yourself up with the remaining leg. Remain for 30 seconds; repeat the other leg. This exercise helps build leg muscle and stretches out the Achilles tendon and calf muscle resulting in a more even foot strike. Importantly, the exercise lends itself to a straighter gait from foot to torso.

- *Check your oxygen intake.* Getting your breath while jogging is a huge challenge for most of us. The basic rule is to begin the jog as slow as your coordination will allow to properly moving one foot in front of the other. Moving too fast may result in breathing to hard prematurely. Practice jogging in a progressive manner, using minutes as your duration signal. Refer to the the schedule given.

- *How does one breathe?* Breathe through your mouth and nose for the most part. Both the breathing in and exhaling out eventually will have steady sound pattern. This "patterned" breathing will make you quite relaxed over time; both physically and mentally.

- *Check your foot strike.* Jogging requires little if any "toe off," but rather a mid-foot strike or better yet, heel to toe. The beginner jogger can deter knee pain and shin splints if a heel to toe strike is initiated during the first month or so, vs. a toeing off. Initially we want our weight deflected toward the back of us vs. the front where both knees and shins are saved from the brunt of full landing impact.

- *What are the first two realistic goals of a beginner jogger or runner?* The 20 minute non-stop jog followed later by a 5K distance. In both cases impact and cardiovascular adaptations will take a few weeks or more to be had.

Week 10
The Calories are Burning

Steady aerobic exercise will change the body in terms of muscular toning, weight, and overall measurements despite the aging process. One certainty of getting older is the fact that our metabolism, or how fast your body burns fuel, slows down. This reality makes it extremely difficult for a sedentary person to lose weight. As we approach our 30's, 40's and beyond, body fat increases as muscle decreases, unless weight bearing plus aerobic exercises are initiated and routinely practiced. Because of the high amount of oxygen consumption it takes to run, our metabolic rate will be higher and energy expenditure will follow.

A general dehydration of cells takes place with the aging process. This means it becomes more critical to drink water before and during exercise, especially when the weather is hot and humid. Also the digestive system slows down resulting in symptoms such as stomach cramps, gas, and constipation. A lifestyle of running and cross training will make the digestive system work more efficiently and help get rid of daily wastes.

Below are effective tips to moderate calorie intake and increase metabolism:

a. *Cut down on the amount of food at night.* And practice a relaxing exercise such as an easy run, walking, or yoga. Your blood sugar levels are highest in the evening. Aerobic exercise like running will neutralize sugar cravings.

b. *Replace sedentary habits with active habits.* Begin taking the stairs, parking further from the store, walk the dog longer, etc. If you run 4-5 days per week, begin to cross-train by practicing weight training, biking, swimming, yoga, etc. This will also give running muscles a rest.

c. *Get stronger and faster.* Practice weight training for your legs and arms and you will not only be moving quicker, but your increased muscle mass will burn more calories throughout the day.

d. *Up your distance and intensity on a monthly basis.* Your metabolism will get used to a set amount of energy expended. Unfortunately the body will get efficient at burning calories and may begin to plateau. Running longer sprinkled in with faster paced workouts increase the metabolic rate.

e. *Follow a healthy eating plan that compliments an active lifestyle versus one that compromises it due to lack of fuel.* Distance exercise like running will not respond to fad diets or any plan that is restrictive with key nutrients.

Week 11
Eating for Energy and Weight Management

Like most things in life worth having, there seem to be sacrifices involved when changing lifelong habits. This is especially true of eating. The quality of life is largely affected by the foods you eat. Proper nutrition paves the way for a slimmer and healthier body; while aerobic exercise helps maintain a slimmer, healthier body. Losing weight or maintaining your desired weight as we age requires lifestyle changes. Altering eating habits and making exercise a part of your lifestyle will definitely help weight management. This necessitates making adjustments with your day to day approach to eating and exercise.

Overeating is caused by practicing a continual pattern of eating wrong foods, eating them too frequently, and not exercising enough for all those extra calories to be expended. The negative aspects of overeating are many. Coronary heart disease due to an overabundance of fat, saturated fat, and cholesterol is the number one killer of women. Diabetes results due to the glucose levels being unregulated and out of control. Hypertension caused by too much sodium results in high blood pressure and is a consequence of too much salt with your eating selections. Then the reality of being obese in itself creates stress on the muscular and skeleton system, not to mention being frustrated by your appearance which can become a self-esteem issue.

There are basic steps the overweight individual can take to subtract the common ailments of heart disease, hypertension, diabetes, and obesity. The first step is to replace wrong foods with right foods. Second, switch non-successful eating habits with time tested habits that aid weight loss. A third step is to control your weight by balancing the calories consumed with the calories expended, by using moderation in eating. Finally, incorporate physical activity to speed up your metabolism, which consequently makes your body able to burn more calories throughout the day.

STEP ONE – Week one: Replace wrong foods with right foods:

Purpose: Gradually wean the cravings away from wrong foods to right foods. Right foods are rich in vitamins and minerals but low in fat, sugar, and salt. Increase your digestion process with fruits and vegetable. The right food choices will provide more accurate "hunger" cues.

Recommendations:

1. Replace all white flour products with whole grain selections. Increased fiber with your grain selections will prompt the digestion system to operate more efficiently.

2. Replace sugar filled foods with fresh fruit and/or dried fruit; limit one small desert per day such as 2 cookies, a small slice of cake, or ½ cup of ice cream.

3. Replace sugar filled cereal with ones with little if any sugar. Try cereals which are whole grain, such as oatmeal.

4. Replace butter and margarine with low-fat, no trans-fat, and use olive oil or other pressed vegetable oils and/or Pam for cooking.

5. Replace regular salad dressing with low-fat salad dressing.

6. Replace high salted foods with those which have less sodium.

7. Replace sitting down activities with outdoor exercise. Put into place an exercise program with at least 60 minutes of aerobic exercise 4-5 days per week.

STEP TWO – Week two: Replace non-successful eating habits with ones which aid weight loss.

Purpose: Changing when and how much you eat will definitely modify food intake and bring upon quicker weight loss.

Recommendations:

1. Snacking is fine, but choose fresh fruit, mixed nuts (without added oil and salt) and dried fruit (without added sugar). Popcorn with Pam cooking spray is acceptable as well. Snacking each two hours or so will keep your energy constant the entire day resulting in less food cravings.

2. Eat a substantial breakfast with protein in it. If it is cereal, add nuts. Remember to drink at least one cup of low fat or skim milk. Protein with breakfast will stabilize blood sugar and will prevent being hungry for most of the morning. Consequently, you will metabolize all food in the morning and not retain excess calories.

3. Lunch should include a large salad with low–fat dressing, protein, 1-2 slices of whole grain bread, plus an optional small desert such as a cookie. Try not to exceed 500 calories for lunch. More than that will result in a sluggish feeling afterwards. Just like in the morning, you will burn all of the calories from lunch until the evening meal since you are still active.

4. Supper should be small and consist mostly of protein and vegetables. You will feel less hungry with a protein filled supper and will burn more calories at night if you eat light. Again snacking is acceptable, such as popcorn, or carrot sticks. Just remember to eat light for your evening meal…a key to weight loss. Practice not eating a few hours before bedtime.

5. Throw out all diet books and do not use the scale anymore. Measure progress by how your clothes fit. Most importantly note the increased energy you have by the end of the second week. Diets do not work in the long term. Rather, an eating plan combined with better eating habits plus exercise will return you back to the proper weight. This statement becomes more valid when you practice food moderation found in Step 3 and exercise in Step 4.

6. Incorporate at least 60 minutes of aerobic exercise for 4-5 days out of the week.

STEP THREE – Week 3 and the rest of your years: Balance your calories with choosing the right foods and corresponding amounts. Practice moderation not elimination.

Purpose: Food choices and moderation make a big difference in how much and how quickly you lose weight. More importantly food moderation must be practiced throughout your life to keep the weight off.

Recommendations:

1. Drink 6-8 glasses of water, especially after eating dried fruits and drinking alcoholic beverages. Both cause dehydration.

2. Increase physical activity to five times a week with 60 min each time of aerobic exercise. Include one cross-training day such as: a strengthening/stretching activity like yoga or light weight-lifting. Aerobic choices include: spinning, biking, swimming, etc.

3. Record eating selections each day. Record keeping makes you more aware of what food you eat and why. In a spiral notebook make 3 columns and label: Time of day, amount eaten, and activity done. Refer to the template in the back of this booklet in appendix #5. Journal recording of food habits will make you more aware of all the food you eat and why. Habits are more successfully changed when we become aware of them. Awareness brings knowledge. Accurate knowledge results in meaningful, long lasting changes. Soon those non-productive habits will be replaced with an active lifestyle which sabotages incorrect food choices.

4. Practice stretching and relaxing at night. Implement at least 2 stretches per evening. If at all possible engage in a yoga class or some type of flexibility class once a week.

5. Each day, read portions of positive thinking books which will help keep you motivated and validate your new permanent lifestyle of health and fitness.

Eating for Energy and Weight Management

Food Group	Daily Servings	Recommended Serving Sizes
Grains:	6-8	1 slice of bread
		1 oz of dry cereal
		½ cup cooked rice
		1 slice of pizza

Importance: Grains are major sources of energy plus the chromium will stabilize blood sugar while providing the necessary fiber for better elimination.

Choices: whole wheat bread, whole wheat or vegetable based pasta, pita bread, bagel, brown rice, unsalted or lightly salted pretzels and popcorn.

Food Group	Daily Servings	Recommended Serving Sizes
Vegetables:		
green vegetables	unlimited	3 cups
color vegetables	4	2 cups
potato – white or sweet	1	1 medium
legumes	2	cups
vegetable juice-low sodium	1	½ cup
tomato sauce-low sodium	1	½ cup

Importance: Vegetables are rich sources of potassium & magnesium which help metabolize the carbohydrates giving you more energy. Vegetables are naturally high in fiber.

Choices: green-broccoli, kale, collards, green beans, spinach, legumes: peas, lima beans, lentils
Color-tomatoes, squash, zucchini, peppers, onions, black olives, mushrooms

Food Group	Daily Servings	Recommended Serving Sizes
Fruits:	6	
fresh fruit, dried		whole fruit, or ½ cup dried
(Dried fruit-no sulfur or added sugar)		
fruit juice	1	½ cup
(fruit juice-no added sugar)		
banana	1	

Importance: Fruits are important sources of energy, magnesium, potassium and fiber.

Choices: apples, grapes, oranges, grapefruit, mangoes, peaches, pineapples, strawberries, tangerines, blueberries Dried fruit: dates, raisins, apricots, etc.

Food Group	Daily Servings	Recommended Serving Sizes
Dairy/Calcium:	2-3	
fat free or low-fat milk		1 cup
low fat yogurt, soy milk,		
protein shake,		
coconut milk,		
almond milk		
non-processed cheese	1	1½ ounce
low-fat cottage cheese	1	½ cup

Importance: Milk products are a major source of protein and calcium which build strong bones, teeth, muscle tissue; plus regulates heartbeat, muscle action and nerve function

Choices: skim milk, low-fat milk, low fat yogurt, frozen yogurt, real whipped cream, protein shakes, Swiss cheese and low sodium mozzarella cheese, low fat ricotta cheese, low fat cottage cheese, other white cheeses (low-sodium)

Food Group	Daily Servings	Recommended Serving Sizes
Protein rich foods:		
lean meats, poultry,	6 or less total	1 oz
poultry, fish, legumes		
tofu, shelled seafood		
eggs	1	1
ravioli, lasagna,	1	½ cup
spaghetti,		
meat-filled casserole		

Importance: Fish is a major source of omega-3 fatty acids. Meat is a major source of iron which improves blood quality and increases resistance to stress and disease. Shelled seafood such as shrimp is a major source of iodine. All the below protein foods are both full of protein & magnesium. Legumes are a rich source of protein and copper which help bone growth; especially valuable for vegetarians.

Choices: all cooked meat & poultry without skin or fat, liver, duck, seafood, black beans, kidney beans, fish, tofu, eggs, legumes: black beans, kidney beans

Food Group	Daily Servings	Recommended Serving Sizes
Nuts and seeds: almonds, walnuts, peanuts, hazelnuts, pecans, soy nuts, sunflower seeds, pumpkin seeds (all low salt)	2-3	½ cup

Importance: Nuts and seeds sustain your energy levels, stabilize your blood sugar. Both almonds and seeds are rich sources of magnesium and manganese. Manganese rich foods help with sex hormone production and are a good source of protein plus fiber.

Choices: almonds, hazelnuts, mixed nuts, peanuts, walnuts, soy nuts, sunflower seeds, pumpkin seeds; no cashews

Food Group	Daily Servings	Recommended Serving Sizes
Fats & Oils: (no trans-fat)	2-3	1 tsp
low fat mayonnaise		1 tbsp
low fat salad dressing		1 tbsp
peanut butter		1 tbsp
green olives		4-5
butter		1 tsp
advocado		1 tbsp

Importance: Fats are a chief storage form of energy in the body; they insulate and protect vital organs plus provide fat-soluble vitamins.

Choices: listed above; no hydrogenated fats or "trans fat" items are to be used. Use "pressed" vegetable oils, low-fat salad dressing with very little if any sugar or salt.

Food Group	Daily Servings	Recommended Serving Sizes
Sweets:	1	
ice cream/sorbet, custard		½
cup cake/pie, ½donut		1 small slice
cookies		2 small
dark chocolate squares		2

Importance: Sweetened foods are usually full of sugar and fat. They have little if any nutrients and use up your natural energy. Refined sugar foods and most sweets can be addictive.

Choices: dark chocolate the darker the better, low fat ice cream or yogurt, cookies without trans-fat

Food Group	Daily Servings	Recommended Serving Sizes
Sports Stuff:		
exercise bar		½ bar
exercise gels		1-3 packets
electrolyte drinks	½ cup	dilute w/ water

Importance: Long periods of aerobic exercise necessitate hydration with electrolyte drinks such as Gatorade. Incorporate carbohydrates plus protein for sustained energy such as Power bars. Gels give additional carbohydrates for an instant "lift" along the way.

Choices: Gatorade, Cytomax, Endurox, Ultima, All Sport, GU, Power Gel, Hammer Gel, Power Bar, Luna Bar…many more choices available

Food Group	Daily Servings	Recommended Serving Sizes
Fun Stuff:		
spirits	1	6 oz glass of wine or beer
diet sodas	1	8 oz
Starbucks	1	1 cup, (low-fat milk)
hot chocolate	1	2 tbsp of cocoa

Importance: Fun foods will keep you sane and "well-balanced" in our society

Choices: endless

Week 12
Record Your Journey

A diary or logbook of your running progress is important for many reasons. It serves as a motivator which reveals the progress made. Journal writing becomes a personal encyclopedia as you record paces, races, and experiences. Information in a somewhat detailed log book will tell how training has developed week after week, and hopefully year after year. What are other benefits of keeping a fitness journal?

- *The record of past experiences can reveal what areas you need to work on in the future.* How did you get to the point of your personal record or best 5K, 10K, or other race event? What distances and pace were most effective?

- *Record keeping is your scoring system for progress made toward distance event goals.* Always record the actual time and/or distance you ran. When pacing a timed portion of the run, record the distance and the time it took. Likewise, when you complete a race, even a 1 mile or 5K time trial, record your actual race time, the date, the temperature, and how you felt.

- *Record weekly or monthly weight and/or measurements.* Long distance running will decrease body fat and reshape your body. Muscle mass will increase weight a bit. Avoid rapid weight loss. Slow, steady weight loss is an indicator of your physical condition since it indicates gaining muscle and gradually losing fat. Remember also each extra pound of weight is equal to five extra pounds put on your knee joints. So practice healthy eating and remember calories do count.

- *Indicate the details of your fitness level.* Physiological indicators such as resting heart rate, maximum heart rate, cholesterol level, insulin levels and body fat are excellent numbers to compare each month or at least each 3 months.

Week 13
Building a Fitness Plan

The idea of initiating an aerobic fitness plan which fits our lifestyle should have specific components or "stages" which will gradually develop both physical strength and aerobic ability. Cardio walking is a great example of a beginner aerobic fitness program since it includes the benefits of muscular development, increased metabolism, and aerobic ability.

Let's look at the steps of putting together a cardio walking fitness plan and the benefits of each stage. This information will help the exercise participant integrate cardio walking into their lifestyle in a practical way, plus the benefits will serve as a continual motivator.

Step 1: Determine the time and the days exercising for an hour can be done. Routine exercise helps the body adapt and give the individual an actual framework to plan their day. It is critical to schedule "rest" days each week so the body can renew strength.

Step 2: Don't put the cart before the horse. The first rule of any exercise involving impact is to get the body in muscular condition. The specific muscles used for cardio walking need to be strengthened. They include: hamstrings, ankles, quadriceps, core, back muscles and arms. Strong muscles surrounding the bones not only protect the bones, but add bone density. A good posture from core and back exercises prevents incorrect form during the "faster moving moments" of cardio-walking.

Step 3: The longer stride of cardio walking or running comes from practicing stretching exercises. An agile walker or runner has a wider stride length which adds to gait efficiency, plus has increased muscle group balance. Equal impact from balanced muscle groups prevent overuse injuries which can occur on the front of the body such as shin splints or as bursitis on the left or right side of the body.

Step 4: Practice the form and technique of cardio walking or running by doing leg lifts and arm lunges each day. Correct posture, forward arm movement and foot strike will result in increased leg and arm efficiency so wasteful movements are eliminated.

Now it's time to "go for a walk" or "go for a run" and implement the ingredients of an aerobic physical fitness plan: Duration, Frequency, Resistance, and Intensity. Get your calendar out and make two goals: A one month goal, and a long term 3 month goal. Here are the basic fitness ingredients which should be part of your cardio walking program.

* *The first month should concentrate on building both distance and frequency of the cardio walk or run.* Typically, one day a week double the average daily distance. Thus, cardio walking for one hour 3 times per week would have one other day where a two hour walk would be done.

Then each week, you can add 10% of your distance time or miles walked per day for gradual muscular adaptation. If the body seems overtired, then change the frequency, or amount of cardio walking/running days.

* *The second month should include a bit of resistance to increase leg strength and gait efficiency.* Pick one day per week and do a workout on hills (parking garage), stair master, or elliptical trainer. Another day of the week adds some aerobic intensity (speed). For example, cardio walk one direction and turn around and return the same direction but a few minutes faster.

* *During third month have fun and take part in the distance event such as a 5K.* If a 5K has already been completed during the first month of training then try to go a bit faster with the second 5K attempt.

Week 14
The Importance of Camaraderie

The importance of camaraderie among women has brought the walk to run events to all-time highs. As a runner, coach, and fitness mentor for many years, I aimed at the fitness angle as a key motivator for women to initiate marathon and half marathon training. Long distance fitness goal(s) results in a lifestyle of fitness, which definitely becomes necessary to walk and/or run either a full marathon or half. Motivation for distance training still focuses on the "fitness angle" but has attached itself to another motivator - support groups. The last few years walk to run training groups have turned into social time on the move. Women stay in their walking or running group for friendship and the "girl talk." So do women need to be convinced to sign up for a distance event for fitness or for the camaraderie? The number one reason for initiating walk to running is the fitness aspect. However the motivation for staying with distance fitness is for the social support. Long term friendships evolve after 3-4 months of training. The act of supporting and nurturing one another evolves into both small and large groups all having a "fitness goal" in mind.

Let's explore together actual research done on women and their need for relationships. Stanford University now offers courses which study the health connection of women and friendship. These courses study the mind-body connection of how women bonding can prevent stress and consequent diseases. The common thread with these collegiate studies reminds women that the most important thing she can do for her health is to "nurture" her relationships with her girlfriends. In other words, women need "girlfriend time" for their overall health. Long distance events guarantee this important support group time.

Furthermore, this "girlfriend" time during distance walking and running creates serotonin – the feel good neurotransmitter which helps women combat depression. Distance exercise also stimulates the release of endorphins which has shown to be a remarkable antidepressant. The mixture of increased serotonin and endorphins from a long bout of aerobic exercise definitely makes an impact on one continuing with their "group."

Group walking and running facilitate support systems that help each other with stressful and challenging life situations. As Andrew Weil mentioned in one of his many articles, the increased usage of internet, e-mail, mobile phones, multimedia, etc. has resulted in a great amount of seclusion and exclusion from the "feeling" world. The technology age subtracts the amount of nurturing words which is how women form relationships. Person to person verbiage is becoming extinct, and social grouping has been transformed in many cases into internet chat rooms.

Enter the game of distance events for women. Now it makes so much sense that our new natural environment of walk to run groups matches thriving natural environments for social group bonding. Distance aerobic exercising not only is doing wonders for our body but creates and maintains quality personal relationships which improve overall mental health.

Week 15
Conquering Common Injuries

As an avid cardio walker or beginner runner who is getting increasingly fit there is generally a desire to increase distance. Extending distance happens for many reasons such as a pinnacle walk event, continuing or maintaining weight loss goals, gaining increased aerobic ability, or other personal distance goals. Increasing time on "the feet" sometimes yields to overuse injuries. Generally speaking, overuse injuries are defined by repetitive use of the weaker tendons, ligaments and/or tight muscles. The obvious cure would be to lessen mileage, cross train, and/or be proactive and engage in a stretching and strength regiment to balance the muscles throughout the body. Having said that, let's see what we can do to fix some of the more common injuries folks on the move face.

Begin with the feet - Distance walking or running results in the feet gaining width. Feet burning, hammertoes, ingrown toes can often be avoided with a wider toe box together with thinner socks. Make sure the socks fit tight so blisters are held at bay. Clip your toenails once a week to prevent ingrown toenails.

Plantar Fasciitis – mostly caused by lack of foot flexibility which results in an overextended fascia- tough, fibrous material stretching from the toes to the heel. Often times fascia gets inflamed when a walker or runner has too much lightness in the shoe allowing the bottom of the foot to overstretch (flex) in the fascia area, which can create pain in the heel. A light shoe together with a forefoot to toe strike can easily overstretch the fascia. The distance walker or runner would be better off with a heavier training shoe for increased stability and decreased flexion ability. Taping the heel for stability will reduce inflammation. Toe raises and calf stretching go a long way to strengthen foot muscles and allow more flexibility in the ankles and calf which can prevent this injury from occurring.

"The Achilles heel" – Achilles tendonitis occurs mostly due to tight calf muscles which then pull the Achilles tendon, the "cord" connecting the heel to the calf muscle, to the point of inflammation. Lengthen the calf muscle by stretching it a few times each day. Put a small ¼" foam heel pad to shorten the distance of the overstretched Achilles.

It's my shins! - Commonly shin splints occur with beginner cardio walkers or runners. The foot strike and body are most likely perched a bit too much forward, making the total weight of the body rest on the shins. Together with the impact of walking, the shins get inflamed and movement becomes extremely painful. If high heels are worn at work, the problem and pain gets increasingly worse. Refine your walking form to a definite heel to toe strike, slightly arch the back so as deflect some body weight toward the back of the body. Ice your shins after each workout. This stretch may seem odd at first but it is quite effective. Point the toes and foot forward and try to pick up objects with them. Or point the foot downward and practice spelling the alphabet with your toes.

Hamstring related injuries – Mostly begin in the glute area and can occur from a number of reasons. Check your hip flexibility. Sit down on a chair crossing one leg over the other and see if you feel a tug in the hip area. Check your leg flexibility. Lie down on the ground; lift one leg up with a rope, keeping the other stationary and see if you can get it perpendicular or straight up in the air. If both tests reveal a tug in the hamstring and/or glute area, it is time to check into hip flexor stretches mentioned above and hamstring stretches described previously.

Week 16
When Do I Cross Train?

It is critical to stay uninjured so the progression of training can be consistent. One effective means of avoiding injuries, especially impact injuries is by cross training. The two major benefits of cross training are immediate. First and most importantly, impact injuries are lessened. Secondly, strength is gained in other muscle areas besides the running muscles. What are some effective cross training exercises which are specifically helpful for the runner?

- *Biking:* gain leg turnover and leg strength without the pounding.

- *Weight Training:* specificity weight training for runners quickens leg turnover while developing strength and improved balance in the legs, the core, and the arms. A strong core/back strengthening program lends itself to improved posture resulting in less frontal impact injuries such as the knee and back.

- *Yoga:* increasing agility in the legs will lengthen the stride resulting in leg economy and less impact. That is just the beginning benefit. Increased balance together with balancing out muscle groups throughout the body help keep an even landing pattern. Consequently one side doesn't have to endure the entire workload.

- *Water running:* this mimics the biomechanics of running without the impact on muscles, joints, and bones. A 30-45 minute workout with music on may actually be one of your choice training days.

- *Walking*: the walking movement uses the same major muscle groups as running but with much lower impact force. A workout could include warming up for 10-20 minutes, and then pick up the walking pace for 10 minutes. Finish with an easy 5 minute walk. Repeat this process 2 more times.

- *Swimming*: will improve flexibility, increase aerobic lung capacity, increase heart rate and decrease muscle inflammation.

When do you have time to cross train? Simply take your rest days and add one or more of the above modalities. Then, eliminate one walk to run day and choose the cross-training you enjoy most and make that an improvement day. Adding cross-training to your walk to run program will most likely give you 4 days of impact versus 5 or 6 days. The body will definitely appreciate the reduced impact.

The future belongs to the beauty of their dreams. Eleanor Roosevelt

<u>**Week Beginning**</u>   /   /
Daily Schedule – Week 9
Miscellaneous Comments

Date	Monday		○
Distance			○
Intensity			○
Cross-			○
Train			○
Weather			

Date	Tuesday		○
Distance			○
Intensity			○
Cross-			○
Train			○
Weather			

Date	Wednesday		○
Distance			○
Intensity			○
Cross-			○
Train			○
Weather			

Date	Thursday		○
Distance			○
Intensity			○
Cross-			○
Train			○
Weather			

Date	Friday		○
Distance			○
Intensity			○
Cross-			○
Train			○
Weather			

Date	Saturday		○
Distance			○
Intensity			○
Cross-			○
Train			○
Weather			

Date	Sunday		○
Distance			○
Intensity			○
Cross-			○
Train			○
Weather			

If we did all things that we are capable of doing, we would literally astound ourselves. Thomas Edison

<u>**Week Beginning**</u>   /   /

Daily Schedule – Week 10
Miscellaneous Comments

Date	Monday		
Distance Intensity Cross- Train Weather		○ ○ ○ ○ ○	——— ——— ——— ——— ———
Date	Tuesday		
Distance Intensity Cross- Train Weather		○ ○ ○ ○ ○	——— ——— ——— ——— ———
Date	Wednesday		
Distance Intensity Cross- Train Weather		○ ○ ○ ○ ○	——— ——— ——— ——— ———
Date	Thursday		
Distance Intensity Cross- Train Weather		○ ○ ○ ○ ○	——— ——— ——— ——— ———
Date	Friday		
Distance Intensity Cross- Train Weather		○ ○ ○ ○ ○	——— ——— ——— ——— ———
Date	Saturday		
Distance Intensity Cross- Train Weather		○ ○ ○ ○ ○	——— ——— ——— ——— ———
Date	Sunday		
Distance Intensity Cross- Train Weather		○ ○ ○ ○ ○	——— ——— ——— ——— ———

It is not length of life, but depth of life. Ralph Waldo Emerson

<u>**Week Beginning**</u>   /   /

Daily Schedule – Week 11

Miscellaneous Comments

Date	Monday		
_____	_____	○	_____
Distance	_____	○	_____
Intensity	_____	○	_____
Cross-	_____	○	_____
Train	_____	○	_____
Weather	_____		
Date	Tuesday		
_____	_____	○	_____
Distance	_____	○	_____
Intensity	_____	○	_____
Cross-	_____	○	_____
Train	_____	○	_____
Weather	_____		
Date	Wednesday		
_____	_____	○	_____
Distance	_____	○	_____
Intensity	_____	○	_____
Cross-	_____	○	_____
Train	_____	○	_____
Weather	_____		
Date	Thursday		
_____	_____	○	_____
Distance	_____	○	_____
Intensity	_____	○	_____
Cross-	_____	○	_____
Train	_____	○	_____
Weather	_____		
Date	Friday		
_____	_____	○	_____
Distance	_____	○	_____
Intensity	_____	○	_____
Cross-	_____	○	_____
Train	_____	○	_____
Weather	_____		
Date	Saturday		
_____	_____	○	_____
Distance	_____	○	_____
Intensity	_____	○	_____
Cross-	_____	○	_____
Train	_____	○	_____
Weather	_____		
Date	Sunday		
_____	_____	○	_____
Distance	_____	○	_____
Intensity	_____	○	_____
Cross-	_____	○	_____
Train	_____	○	_____
Weather	_____		

What we learn to do, we learn by doing. Thomas Jefferson

Week Beginning _____ / _____ / _____
Daily Schedule – Week 12
Miscellaneous Comments

Date	Monday		
		○	_____
		○	_____
Distance		○	_____
Intensity		○	_____
Cross-Train		○	_____
Weather			

Date	Tuesday		
		○	_____
		○	_____
Distance		○	_____
Intensity		○	_____
Cross-Train		○	_____
Weather			

Date	Wednesday		
		○	_____
		○	_____
Distance		○	_____
Intensity		○	_____
Cross-Train		○	_____
Weather			

Date	Thursday		
		○	_____
		○	_____
Distance		○	_____
Intensity		○	_____
Cross-Train		○	_____
Weather			

Date	Friday		
		○	_____
		○	_____
Distance		○	_____
Intensity		○	_____
Cross-Train		○	_____
Weather			

Date	Saturday		
		○	_____
		○	_____
Distance		○	_____
Intensity		○	_____
Cross-Train		○	_____
Weather			

Date	Sunday		
		○	_____
		○	_____
Distance		○	_____
Intensity		○	_____
Cross-Train		○	_____
Weather			

It is not in the stars to hold our destiny, but in ourselves. William Shakespeare

<u>Week Beginning</u>   /   /

Daily Schedule – Week 13

Miscellaneous Comments

Date	Monday		
		○	_____
		○	_____
Distance		○	_____
Intensity		○	_____
Cross-Train		○	_____
Weather			
Date	Tuesday		
		○	_____
		○	_____
Distance		○	_____
Intensity		○	_____
Cross-Train		○	_____
Weather			
Date	Wednesday		
		○	_____
		○	_____
Distance		○	_____
Intensity		○	_____
Cross-Train		○	_____
Weather			
Date	Thursday		
		○	_____
		○	_____
Distance		○	_____
Intensity		○	_____
Cross-Train		○	_____
Weather			
Date	Friday		
		○	_____
		○	_____
Distance		○	_____
Intensity		○	_____
Cross-Train		○	_____
Weather			
Date	Saturday		
		○	_____
		○	_____
Distance		○	_____
Intensity		○	_____
Cross-Train		○	_____
Weather			
Date	Sunday		
		○	_____
		○	_____
Distance		○	_____
Intensity		○	_____
Cross-Train		○	_____
Weather			

Example isn't another way to teach, it is the only way to teach. Albert Einstein

Week Beginning   /   /
Daily Schedule – Week 14
Miscellaneous Comments

Date	Monday		
Distance		○	
Intensity		○	
Cross-		○	
Train		○	
Weather		○	

Date	Tuesday		
Distance		○	
Intensity		○	
Cross-		○	
Train		○	
Weather		○	

Date	Wednesday		
Distance		○	
Intensity		○	
Cross-		○	
Train		○	
Weather		○	

Date	Thursday		
Distance		○	
Intensity		○	
Cross-		○	
Train		○	
Weather		○	

Date	Friday		
Distance		○	
Intensity		○	
Cross-		○	
Train		○	
Weather		○	

Date	Saturday		
Distance		○	
Intensity		○	
Cross-		○	
Train		○	
Weather		○	

Date	Sunday		
Distance		○	
Intensity		○	
Cross-		○	
Train		○	
Weather		○	

The greatest discovery of my generation is that a human being can alter his life by altering his attitudes. William James

<u>**Week Beginning**</u>   **/**   **/**
Daily Schedule – Week 15
Miscellaneous Comments

Date	Monday		
		○	_____
___		○	_____
Distance		○	_____
Intensity		○	_____
Cross-Train		○	_____
Weather			
Date	Tuesday		
		○	_____
___		○	_____
Distance		○	_____
Intensity		○	_____
Cross-Train		○	_____
Weather			
Date	Wednesday		
		○	_____
___		○	_____
Distance		○	_____
Intensity		○	_____
Cross-Train		○	_____
Weather			
Date	Thursday		
		○	_____
___		○	_____
Distance		○	_____
Intensity		○	_____
Cross-Train		○	_____
Weather			
Date	Friday		
		○	_____
___		○	_____
Distance		○	_____
Intensity		○	_____
Cross-Train		○	_____
Weather			
Date	Saturday		
		○	_____
___		○	_____
Distance		○	_____
Intensity		○	_____
Cross-Train		○	_____
Weather			
Date	Sunday		
		○	_____
___		○	_____
Distance		○	_____
Intensity		○	_____
Cross-Train		○	_____
Weather			

I like nonsense. It wakes up the brain cells. Fantasy is a necessary ingredient in living; it's a way of looking at life through the wrong end of a telescope. Dr. Seuss

Week Beginning   /   /
Daily Schedule – Week 16
Miscellaneous Comments

Date	Monday		
Distance		○	
Intensity		○	
Cross-Train		○	
Weather		○	

Date	Tuesday		
Distance		○	
Intensity		○	
Cross-Train		○	
Weather		○	

Date	Wednesday		
Distance		○	
Intensity		○	
Cross-Train		○	
Weather		○	

Date	Thursday		
Distance		○	
Intensity		○	
Cross-Train		○	
Weather		○	

Date	Friday		
Distance		○	
Intensity		○	
Cross-Train		○	
Weather		○	

Date	Saturday		
Distance		○	
Intensity		○	
Cross-Train		○	
Weather		○	

Date	Sunday		
Distance		○	
Intensity		○	
Cross-Train		○	
Weather		○	

Phase 3
Jog to Run

Duration Training

Weeks 17 – 24

Weeks 17 - 24
Intensity and Stamina Training

Notes: Set half marathon and/or marathon pace per mile
Do one 5k per month on Saturday or Sunday
Choose your goal time and distance from Appendix 7
Pick the fitness level you currently are at and follow the tempo and track workouts found
in Appendix 6

a/m/m = the average minutes per mile at an easy effort
aerobic running = goal mile pace for half and/or whole marathon event
tempo running = 20 seconds per mile faster than goal pace

Weeks 17 - 18:

Levels	Monday	Tuesday	Wednesday	Thursday	Friday	Saturday	Sunday
Beginner: Walk & jog (14-16 a/m/m)	Conditioning Exercises	Track w/o 1 mile of intervals	off	Tempo w/o 2 miles of tempo	c/t or rest	3 miles easy walk & jog HILLS	6 miles easy walk & jog
Intermediate: Jogger (11 – 13 a/m/m)	Conditioning Exercises	Track w/o 1.5 miles of intervals	30 min. aerobic running	Tempo w/o 3 miles of tempo	c/t or rest	3 miles easy jog HILLS	7-8 miles easy jog
Advanced: Runner (7 – 10 a/m/m)	Conditioning Exercises	Track w/o 2 miles of intervals	30 min. aerobic running	Tempo w/o 4 miles of tempo	c/t or rest	5 miles easy jog HILLS	8-9 miles easy run

Weeks 19 - 20:

Levels	Monday	Tuesday	Wednesday	Thursday	Friday	Saturday	Sunday
Beginner: Walk & jog (14-16 a/m/m)	Conditioning Exercises	Track w/o 1 mile of intervals	30 min. aerobic running	Tempo w/o 2 miles of tempo	c/t or rest	3 miles easy walk & jog	8 miles easy walk & jog HILLS
Intermediate: Jogger (11 – 13 a/m/m)	Conditioning Exercises	Track w/o 2 miles of intervals	30 min. aerobic running	Tempo w/o 4 miles of tempo	c/t or rest	3 miles easy jog	10 miles easy jog HILLS
Advanced: Runner (7 – 10 a/m/m)	Conditioning Exercises	Track w/o 2.5 miles of intervals	45 min. aerobic running	Tempo w/o 5 miles of tempo	c/t or rest	5 miles easy jog	10 – 13 miles easy run HILLS

Weeks 21 – 22:

Levels	Monday	Tuesday	Wednesday	Thursday	Friday	Saturday	Sunday
Beginner: Walk & jog (14-16 a/m/m)	Conditioning Exercises	Track w/o 1 mile of intervals	30 min. aerobic running	Tempo w/o 3 miles of tempo	c/t or rest	3 miles easy walk & jog HILLS	10 miles easy walk & jog
Intermediate: Jogger (11 – 13 a/m/m)	Conditioning Exercises	Track w/o 2 miles of intervals	45 min. aerobic running	Tempo w/o 5 miles of tempo	c/t or rest	3 miles easy jog HILLS	12 miles easy jog
Advanced: Runner (7 – 10 a/m/m)	Conditioning Exercises	Track w/o 2.5 miles of intervals	55 min. aerobic running	Tempo w/o 6 miles of tempo	c/t or rest	5 miles easy jog HILLS	13 – 15 miles easy run

Weeks 23 - 24:

Levels	Monday	Tuesday	Wednesday	Thursday	Friday	Saturday	Sunday
Beginner: Walk & jog (14-16 a/m/m)	Conditioning Exercises	Track w/o 1 mile of intervals	30 min. aerobic running	Tempo w/o 3 miles of tempo	c/t or rest	3 miles easy walk & jog	12 miles easy walk & jog HILLS
Intermediate: Jogger (11 – 13 a/m/m)	Conditioning Exercises	Track w/o 2 miles of intervals	45 min. aerobic running	Tempo w/o 6 miles of tempo	c/t or rest	3 miles easy jog	13 miles easy jog HILLS
Advanced: Runner (7 – 10 a/m/m)	Conditioning Exercises	Track w/o 2.5 miles of intervals	60 min. aerobic running	Tempo w/o 8 miles of tempo	c/t or rest	5 miles easy jog	15 -18 miles easy run HILLS

Week 17
Striders – Weight Training for Runners

Striders are short bouts of running and are no longer than 100 yards in length. One main benefit of striders is they allow one to practice correct running form at a quicker pace. To improve the economy of movement, runners should practice using correct biomechanics while moving at a faster pace. A big advantage from doing striders is the strengthening effect. Doing 4 -5 striders after a workout serve to teach the muscles to turn over fast despite their fatigue. Strider practice transfers nicely for race simulation since most of us will have leg tiredness toward the end and experiencing the "hitting the wall" effect before the race ends. However, strider practice will help keep you on goal pace toward the finish line. Lastly, striding does help recruit the fast twitch muscles. Simply put, to run faster one must have leg muscles which are trained to respond with more rapid turnover. Striders together with other forms of speed work mentioned later will help sustain a pace increase for the duration of your goal event.

Some striding guidelines:

* *Do striders on a level surface* whenever possible since an even foot strike is an integral part of good form.

* *Divide the 100 yard length into 3 equal parts*: slow jog pacing, then pick it up to a full stride run pace, and complete the last part at a 5K or faster pace. In sum: 70%, 85%, then full out 95-100% effort

* *The amount of striders varies according to the workout planned.* Here are three strider scenarios: Advanced runners can go up to 20 striders as part of a form workout. Six to eight striders can be mixed in during an easy 3-5 mile run. For the "weight training" effect, follow your easy effort runs with 4 to 5 striders.

* *Each strider is done with an equal movement of legs and arms* working together for forward motion. After each strider a rest of 30 seconds is recommended so the optimal running form can be repeated.

* *The important part of the strider is to practice a "toe off"* upon the initiation of the last part when a 95% effort is employed. This "toe off" or forefoot strike helps tremendously in 5K's and for a quick "finish line" ending.

Note: Be sure your calves and Achilles are properly stretched before doing striders.

Week 18
Bounding for Leg Strength

Bounding is a pronounced leg lift while moving slightly forward. This leg lift technique is best done on soft surface. The main point of the exaggerated lifting of the legs is to develop leg turnover plus strengthen all the leg muscles used while running, especially hill running. What does a bounding workout consist of?

- *Find a soft surface and develop an easy run to bounding ratio before starting off.* For example, do 3 minutes to 30 seconds for 2 miles. That ratio translates to 3 minutes easy run with regular stride, and then on purpose practice high leg lifting for 30 seconds. Continue that pattern until your mileage is reached. When bounding, your forward motion will be reduced since the legs are going more upward.

- *Bounding can be done prior to a track workout.* Bounding helps with quick leg turnover and prepares your leg muscles for ballistic fast movement, thus becoming a good warm-up for a track session.

- *Practice bounding the day after a long run, again on soft surface.* Long distance runners benefit from easy running the day after a long run since their legs are tired. A bounding ratio workout like the one mentioned above is a great way to build leg strength because of the two resistances built in the workout prior to beginning. The first resistance is the fact your legs are tired and the second one is the lifting legs up higher than your normal stride. Remember, a soft surface is necessary to avoid impact injuries.

Week 19
The Four Paces of Eve

There is a time in distance training when the training ingredient of stamina or long distance speed can be added. Weekly stamina workouts can be added after your "base" mileage has been stabilized and the body has adapted aerobically and physically to goal base mileage training. Listed below are the most commonly used stamina workouts and the rationale for distance runners. (refer to Appendix 6 for a variety of track and tempo workouts)

- *Track intervals*: will increase leg turnover and efficiency plus develop increased lung capacity. Distance runners should aim for the ½ mile or 1 mile repeats since it is more specific to their distance goals. As a rule, track repeats are run at 95% effort or slightly faster than 5K goal pace, with the rest intervals lasting an equal amount of time with an easy jog.

- *Fartlek or tempo running*: Fartlek is the Swedish term for "speed play," and is also termed as tempo running in this manual. In each case, one runs intermittently at an 85% effort for a certain distance or amount of minutes, than slowing down to an easy pace for a certain distance or time. A ratio can be developed or just alternate effort levels as you are running.

- *Why practice tempo running*? You will learn to be a more consistent runner who knows how to judge a realistic "faster" pace throughout the duration of the run.

- *What actually is a tempo run*? A steady pace of five or more minutes at a comfortably hard effort or about 10-20 seconds faster than your long distance goal pace. Therefore if you plan to run a 9 minute per mile for your goal 5K race, you would practice running at an 8:45 minute mile pace. Of course longer running goals such as a half marathon necessitate a longer practice workout.

- *How do you begin a tempo run*? Go out easy for one half a mile, then pick out a short distance such as a quarter mile and run that at your tempo pace. Then slow down for 3 minutes, and continue the quarter mile of 3 minute easy to tempo ratio three or more times. Longer distances would require more repetitions of a given ratio.

- *Long distance "pushes"*: are usually done every other week and are implemented to simulate long distance faster running for distance runners. Implementing bi-monthly "pushes" just under the pre-determined long distance goal race pace will help facilitate faster goal finish time and reduce the "dead leg" feeling toward the end. Marathoners should get up to at least a 13 mile push before their event and half marathoners up to

10 miles. Half marathon events are perfect for doing "pushes" for marathon training as long as the pace is controlled and not all out.

- *Hill repeats* – will exponentially increase leg power and speed which give both legs and arms tremendous strength. Distance runners who do hill repeats have an advantage from those who do not. As the length of the run progresses and the legs begin to tire, hill runners avoid early tiredness and can maintain more of a push toward the end. The hill should be a similar elevation as you would see on a highway overpass, generally more than one quarter mile in length.

What can you expect after a month or two of faster paced sessions?

- Lactate threshold will increase despite running at a faster speed
- Aerobic capacity will increase
- Race times will reduce due to increased overall stamina, leg efficiency, and increased aerobic capacity
- By becoming a more efficient runner, you will economize on energy demands while running faster at further distances
- Fueling on "pushes" will teach the body to process and digest energy supported bars and/or liquids while having a higher heart rate

Week 20
The Hills are Alive

Hill training will add significant strength to the legs, especially the quadriceps and hamstrings. Running hills increases up and down leg motion which translates into becoming a faster runner. Finding a hilly course adds variety to the running regiment. Hill training is usually done in the beginning stages of long distance training because of the strength added to the legs.

What if there are no hills near where you live? A few alternatives are parking garages and climbing stairs. Try an office building or stadium steps if available. The stair climbing machine in a gym is also a viable choice. Below are the benefits of hill training.

- *Uphills will improve form:* lean back when going uphill, shorten and heighten your stride. This results in strengthening both quads and hamstrings.

- *Downhill running will improve leg speed*: As you head down a hill, bend down at the pelvis slightly and use your same foot strike as you do on the flat ground. Allow gravity to do its' job so you can achieve a quicker pace. *Caution:* The hill cannot be too steep, nor can this training be done too frequently since it is stressful on the knees and shins. You can do hill training once a week maximum. If you are training on steep down hills, it is better to arch the back, go down heel to toe and lead with the chest to subtract the impact on the front of the legs.

- *Hill training is speedwork in disguise*: The continual pitter patter of high leg lifting and short steps makes you get into an anaerobic state by the time you reach the top of a quarter mile hill. In other words you are breathless at the crest, which is the same feeling one gets after doing a 400 yard repeat on the track.

- *Hills will strengthen both quads and hamstrings*: Leg strength will help prevent running injuries to the lower parts of your legs, such as the calves and knees. Just remember to use proper uphill and downhill form.

- *Smile when seeing a hill:* When a race event has hills, the hills will become an advantage. Your legs will have learned to bound right up and race down each hill. Smile as you pass those who trained on flat ground only.

Week 21
Duration is Key

Long runs or duration runs are mostly associated with half and marathon distances. How does this infamous long weekend run make you a stronger long distance runner? Physiologically speaking the long run increases the number of mitochondria and capillaries in the active muscles, thus improving the muscles' ability to remove and utilize available oxygen. Also the long run will recruit muscle fibers that would otherwise go unused. The increase in muscle fibers gets "conditioned" and will be there for you to use during the later stages of long distance run. Psychologically speaking, mental toughness is gained when you actually run the goal distance or more. Given this rationale let's consider a few more principles to apply to the long distance run.

- *What is the main purpose of the long run?* Simply put, it is a dress rehearsal for your race; you practice drinking fluids and taking in foods which the body will practice turning into energy. Most importantly, the long run conditions the muscles to delay overall muscle fatigue.

- *What is the best long-run training distance to race/or finish a half marathon and marathon distance?*

  1/2 marathon - 14-18 miles every other week - race
       8-10 miles every third week – to finish
  Marathon - 20-24 miles every other week with one 26 miler – race
       18-20 miles every third week – to finish

Note: For reaching your best aerobic potential, each long run should be practiced six to eight times before your goal race. Also beginners should take walking breaks during their drink stations; experienced runners can stop each 2 miles for a drink and continue onward.

- *How fast should I run the long runs?* Speed is of limited importance during long runs; especially when it is warm. An additional two minutes per mile can be added to the long run. The time on your feet is the critical factor. Better to err going slower than faster. As you gain experience, strength, and confidence of the distance, you can increase the speed the last few miles. Remember, going fast on long runs decreases the quality of the other workout days. Running continually on overworked muscles will lead to injury.

- *How much recovery do I need after long runs?* For at least two days afterwards you should run fairly easy. As your conditioning increases, long runs are less stressful physically and mentally which will enable an increased recovery rate.

- *Are there any tricks to quicken recovery?* Yes, drink a protein/carbohydrate drink within 15 minutes. Put ice water on your legs. Repeat this recovery regiment again in the evening.

Week 22
Eating on the Run

Distance runners will need to replenish carbohydrates while on the run. The question really becomes one of digestion. Which foods, gels, energy bars, and liquids can you not only swallow but fully digest while on the move? First, consider eating an easily digestible light carbohydrate snack an hour before hitting the road. Then consider what will keep blood glucose up or your "fuel tank" full while training.

- *First consider the type of workout.* Fast, short intervals on the track require less bulky food since your digestive system is compromised due to lack of oxygen. In this case water with a bit of electrolyte should do. When walking or running long distances, learn what food can give the sustained energy your body requires to keep blood glucose levels up.

- *Consider the intensity of the workout.* Long stamina workouts such as tempo running or pushes will require food replacement. Remember, simple carbohydrate fuel sources digest better while moving fast since both the metabolic rate and breathing rate are challenged making full digestion near to impossible. Practice with gels or gel bites for example to see if you can digest this fuel replacement while moving at a faster than normal pace.

- *Consider the frequency of all workouts per week.* If you are increasing mileage as the weeks dictate on your schedule, a standard diet will necessitate more complex carbohydrates and protein to sustain the energy put out on the roads.

- *Consider what to drink or eat after the run.* Studies show that a carbohydrate drink with protein will not only replace your glucose levels quicker but help with muscle repair. Again, find a carbohydrate/protein drink you can tolerate, and then drink it within fifteen minutes following the workout. Follow with hydration of water throughout the day.

Week 23
Heat, Humidity and Long Distance

A chief environmental concern and challenge for distance runners is learning to run in the heat. Both walkers and runners who train in the heat must consider first their heart rate will be higher than usual. Heat will challenge the cardiovascular system since it must maintain a cardiac output to match the needs of the muscles which are already increasing their blood flow. Also, hydration is critical to replace the sweat produced which together will help regulate the internal body temperature. Distance runners could be faced with not only heat, but high humidity which also heightens core temperatures and increases the heart rate. Heat and humidity together make sweat barely evaporate, which greatly subtracts your internal cooling system. Lastly, training in the heat day after day increases the body's temperature day by day. Consequently even though you may have cooled off from the previous day's track workout, you still will be more "warmed" up the next day of training. All these factors must be considered to avoid heat related problems such as heat exhaustion. What are ways in which the runner can adapt and manage their training despite daily heat and humidity?

- *The infamous "seven to seven" rule should be followed.* Run before 7:00 am or after 7:00pm. In other words, run without the sun beating on you and run during the coolest part of the day.

- *Continuous replenishment of water while running and sweating.* Distance runners should drink at least 8 ounces of cool water every 10-20 minutes or so with a bit of electrolyte replacement or salt tablets if tolerated. Forget warm water; cool water empties more rapidly from the stomach into the intestines where it can be absorbed.

- *Allow sweat to evaporate.* Wear light colors which reflect heat rather than dark colors. Fabrics are now available which wick perspiration away from the body quickly.

- *Be prepared to go slower during the summer and on days when the temperature exceeds 70 degrees.* Stop for fluid replacement each two miles or so; especially on long run days.

- *Medicines and alcohol can worsen the experience with heat.* Many medicines are diuretics which subtract fluid and increase the heart rate. Alcohol dilates your blood vessels making them less able to protect your body's temperature when the outside air is hot.

Know the signs of the three most frequent types of heat illnesses:

Heat cramps: painful muscle spasms in large muscle groups such as the calves
Heat exhaustion: profuse sweating together with electrolyte loss produces a drop in blood pressure resulting in early fatigue, nausea, lightheadedness, severe headaches, high heart rate, and possible fainting
Heat stroke: a heat overload together with the body's inability to lower its' temperature; signs are dizziness, high body temperature, and dry skin due to lack of sweating.

Week 24
My Feet are Hurting

Before taking the first steps in a walk to run distance program, the selection of the correct running shoe is of critical importance. Generally when the feet are ailing, other parts of the body will follow, so take note before your feet do. It is crucial to wear the correct shoe. Distance runners and walkers alike do well with a stable, cushioned trainer; wide enough in the toe box to allow the foot to have the room it needs. A cushioned, stability training shoe is of great value to women since their hips carry their body and therefore foot strike a bit over to the outside-called supination or to the inside called pronation. A slightly wider toe box is an advantage since there is a bit of swelling after a long workout and after time, your feet will increase in width.

What are the common ailments and remedies for our feet during the long distance journey?

- *Achilles tendonitis*: calf muscle tightness which extends to the Achilles tendon. Take an anti-inflammatory such as ibuprofen, do frequent ice massages, and place a quarter inch heel lift in the running shoe and dress shoe. Allow a few days off of running to lessen the inflammation, then gradually go at it again.

- *Blisters:* prolonged friction between foot, socks, and shoe. Do not wear cotton socks, but instead purchase moisture wicking socks; preferably thin socks if you live in the South. Swab the blister with alcohol; prick it with a needle heated in a flame. Drain, and then cover with an adhesive bandage. After 48 hours, allow air to hit it.

- *Hammertoes:* results from a misalignment of the foot. This causes excessive overpronation, making the tendons of the toe pull and bend at an angle causing a corn to gradually develop. Solutions are the following: try a motion control shoe first and then check to see if the running shoes give your toes enough room to move. If all else fails, look into getting an orthotic made.

- *Ingrown toenails:* occur because shoes are too tight or failure to clip the toes regularly. Clean up the toe by clipping out that which is growing inside your skin. Use peroxide and keep the toe very clean the next few days.

- *Metatarsalgia:* occurs behind the foot metatarsal area when the ball of the foot becomes bruised due to continual direct impact. The best way to treat it is to raise the area around the swelling with moleskin padding material. Reduce the pain in this area by cutting a hole in the insole of your shoe directly under the painful metatarsal. This condition is best prevented by a wider toe box in your running shoe.

- *Prevention of foot injuries:* stay with a wide toe box so your feet can spread out naturally. Devices to alleviate strain and stress to the feet while running should be mimicked at work as well. Alternate running shoes every other day. Avoid high heels especially after your long run since the may create shin splints. Lastly, try to run on soft surfaces at least one time per week; more would be better.

Week 25
Say HI to Hydration

Many distance runners dislike stopping for water since it slows down their pace and net time. However there are more benefits than not by hydrating on the way. First and foremost keep drinking water during the day so that your body is not on empty going into the run. We tend to drink coffee, soda, and other diuretic drinks which eliminate needed electrolytes and minerals. Drinking water with a bit of electrolyte replacement during the day and during the run resolves dehydration issues. But let's get back to the question, what are the benefits of hydration?

- *Water keeps your muscles supple and your joints more flexible.* Given a cold day, water actually keeps your internal organs and muscles warmer.

- *Water cools you off on a warm, humid and/or hot day.* Developing a sweat is great since it provides a way for your body to cool; however you need water to replace the amount that you lose through sweat.

- *Water prevents dehydration and heat exhaustion.* Drinking water and splashing it on the back of your neck and arms will cool you down quickly. Wear a tennis sweat band, and on your various stops hydrate it with cold water and squeeze water on your body as you are running.

- *Water breaks give you an excuse to cool off on the run.* Running when you are hot and getting overheated is not a pleasant experience and combined with not drinking, you are putting yourself at risk for heat related illness. The remedy is to stop, drink, cool off and continue.

- *Long distance runners should practice hydrating while on the move.* The actual half marathon or marathon distance supports runners with water and electrolyte replacement every mile or two. In warm or hot conditions your body can perform only as good as it can hold water and use for cooling.

- *Runners may be concerned if there is no water on their long runs.* Drive the planned course the night before or morning of and place water and electrolyte replacement drinks in various places on your course; ideally every two miles.

- *Caution* – water intoxication known as *hyponatremia* can occur among distance runners if they drink too much water while walking or running. Taking in large amounts of water without sweating much can affect the brain function causing one to collapse or become dizzy and confused. The body's normal balance of electrolytes or sodium is literally pushed out of the body, and not being replenished properly by just water.

Pain is inevitable, but misery is optional. Time Hansel, author

<u>Week Beginning</u>   /   /
Daily Schedule – Week 17
Miscellaneous Comments

Date	Monday		
———		○	———————
Distance		○	———————
Intensity		○	———————
Cross-		○	———————
Train		○	———————
Weather			
Date	Tuesday		
———		○	———————
Distance		○	———————
Intensity		○	———————
Cross-		○	———————
Train		○	———————
Weather			
Date	Wednesday		
———		○	———————
Distance		○	———————
Intensity		○	———————
Cross-		○	———————
Train		○	———————
Weather			
Date	Thursday		
———		○	———————
Distance		○	———————
Intensity		○	———————
Cross-		○	———————
Train		○	———————
Weather			
Date	Friday		
———		○	———————
Distance		○	———————
Intensity		○	———————
Cross-		○	———————
Train		○	———————
Weather			
Date	Saturday		
———		○	———————
Distance		○	———————
Intensity		○	———————
Cross-		○	———————
Train		○	———————
Weather			
Date	Sunday		
———		○	———————
Distance		○	———————
Intensity		○	———————
Cross-		○	———————
Train		○	———————
Weather			

If you don't know where you are going, you might wind up somewhere else. Yogi Berra

Week Beginning / /
Daily Schedule – Week 18
Miscellaneous Comments

Date	Monday		
Distance Intensity Cross-Train Weather		○ ○ ○ ○ ○	_____
Date	**Tuesday**		
Distance Intensity Cross-Train Weather		○ ○ ○ ○ ○	_____
Date	**Wednesday**		
Distance Intensity Cross-Train Weather		○ ○ ○ ○ ○	_____
Date	**Thursday**		
Distance Intensity Cross-Train Weather		○ ○ ○ ○ ○	_____
Date	**Friday**		
Distance Intensity Cross-Train Weather		○ ○ ○ ○ ○	_____
Date	**Saturday**		
Distance Intensity Cross-Train Weather		○ ○ ○ ○ ○	_____
Date	**Sunday**		
Distance Intensity Cross-Train Weather		○ ○ ○ ○ ○	_____

The only time you lose is when you quit. Mike Dunleavy

Week Beginning _____/_____/_____
Daily Schedule – Week 19
Miscellaneous Comments

Date	Monday		
_____		○	_____
		○	_____
Distance	_____	○	_____
Intensity	_____	○	_____
Cross-Train	_____	○	_____
Weather	_____		
Date	**Tuesday**		
_____		○	_____
		○	_____
Distance	_____	○	_____
Intensity	_____	○	_____
Cross-Train	_____	○	_____
Weather	_____		
Date	**Wednesday**		
_____		○	_____
		○	_____
Distance	_____	○	_____
Intensity	_____	○	_____
Cross-Train	_____	○	_____
Weather	_____		
Date	**Thursday**		
_____		○	_____
		○	_____
Distance	_____	○	_____
Intensity	_____	○	_____
Cross-Train	_____	○	_____
Weather	_____		
Date	**Friday**		
_____		○	_____
		○	_____
Distance	_____	○	_____
Intensity	_____	○	_____
Cross-Train	_____	○	_____
Weather	_____		
Date	**Saturday**		
_____		○	_____
		○	_____
Distance	_____	○	_____
Intensity	_____	○	_____
Cross-Train	_____	○	_____
Weather	_____		
Date	**Sunday**		
_____		○	_____
		○	_____
Distance	_____	○	_____
Intensity	_____	○	_____
Cross-Train	_____	○	_____
Weather	_____		

If you don't dream it, you can't become it. Magic Johnson

<u>Week Beginning</u>   /   /
Daily Schedule – Week 20
Miscellaneous Comments

Date	Monday		
———		○	_____
Distance	_____	○	_____
Intensity	_____	○	_____
Cross-	_____	○	_____
Train	_____	○	_____
Weather	_____		
Date	**Tuesday**		
———		○	_____
Distance	_____	○	_____
Intensity	_____	○	_____
Cross-	_____	○	_____
Train	_____	○	_____
Weather	_____		
Date	**Wednesday**		
———		○	_____
Distance	_____	○	_____
Intensity	_____	○	_____
Cross-	_____	○	_____
Train	_____	○	_____
Weather	_____		
Date	**Thursday**		
———		○	_____
Distance	_____	○	_____
Intensity	_____	○	_____
Cross-	_____	○	_____
Train	_____	○	_____
Weather	_____		
Date	**Friday**		
———		○	_____
Distance	_____	○	_____
Intensity	_____	○	_____
Cross-	_____	○	_____
Train	_____	○	_____
Weather	_____		
Date	**Saturday**		
———		○	_____
Distance	_____	○	_____
Intensity	_____	○	_____
Cross-	_____	○	_____
Train	_____	○	_____
Weather	_____		
Date	**Sunday**		
———		○	_____
Distance	_____	○	_____
Intensity	_____	○	_____
Cross-	_____	○	_____
Train	_____	○	_____
Weather	_____		

I decided to be the best and the smartest. Oprah Winfrey

<u>**Week Beginning**</u>　　　／　　　／
Daily Schedule – Week 21
Miscellaneous Comments

Date	Monday		
Distance Intensity Cross- Train Weather		○ ○ ○ ○ ○	
Date	Tuesday		
Distance Intensity Cross- Train Weather		○ ○ ○ ○ ○	
Date	Wednesday		
Distance Intensity Cross- Train Weather		○ ○ ○ ○ ○	
Date	Thursday		
Distance Intensity Cross- Train Weather		○ ○ ○ ○ ○	
Date	Friday		
Distance Intensity Cross- Train Weather		○ ○ ○ ○ ○	
Date	Saturday		
Distance Intensity Cross- Train Weather		○ ○ ○ ○ ○	
Date	Sunday		
Distance Intensity Cross- Train Weather		○ ○ ○ ○ ○	

Life should be a world's fair of delights. Walt Disney

<u>Week Beginning</u>   /   /
Daily Schedule – Week 22
Miscellaneous Comments

Date	Monday		
Distance Intensity Cross-Train Weather		○ ○ ○ ○ ○	___ ___ ___ ___ ___
Date	Tuesday		
Distance Intensity Cross-Train Weather		○ ○ ○ ○ ○	___ ___ ___ ___ ___
Date	Wednesday		
Distance Intensity Cross-Train Weather		○ ○ ○ ○ ○	___ ___ ___ ___ ___
Date	Thursday		
Distance Intensity Cross-Train Weather		○ ○ ○ ○ ○	___ ___ ___ ___ ___
Date	Friday		
Distance Intensity Cross-Train Weather		○ ○ ○ ○ ○	___ ___ ___ ___ ___
Date	Saturday		
Distance Intensity Cross-Train Weather		○ ○ ○ ○ ○	___ ___ ___ ___ ___
Date	Sunday		
Distance Intensity Cross-Train Weather		○ ○ ○ ○ ○	___ ___ ___ ___ ___

Every day you aren't getting stronger and better, you are getting weaker and worse.
D.A. Benton

Week Beginning _____ / _____ / _____

Daily Schedule – Week 23

Miscellaneous Comments

Date	Monday		
Distance **Intensity** **Cross- Train** **Weather**		○ ○ ○ ○ ○	
Date	Tuesday		
Distance **Intensity** **Cross- Train** **Weather**		○ ○ ○ ○ ○	
Date	Wednesday		
Distance **Intensity** **Cross- Train** **Weather**		○ ○ ○ ○ ○	
Date	Thursday		
Distance **Intensity** **Cross- Train** **Weather**		○ ○ ○ ○ ○	
Date	Friday		
Distance **Intensity** **Cross- Train** **Weather**		○ ○ ○ ○ ○	
Date	Saturday		
Distance **Intensity** **Cross- Train** **Weather**		○ ○ ○ ○ ○	
Date	Sunday		
Distance **Intensity** **Cross- Train** **Weather**		○ ○ ○ ○ ○	

As one goes through life, one learns that if you don't paddle your own canoe, you don't move. Katherine Hepburn

Week Beginning ____/____/____

Daily Schedule – Week 24

Miscellaneous Comments

Date	Monday		
		○	_____
		○	_____
Distance	_____	○	_____
Intensity	_____	○	_____
Cross-	_____	○	_____
Train	_____		
Weather	_____		
Date	Tuesday		
		○	_____
		○	_____
Distance	_____	○	_____
Intensity	_____	○	_____
Cross-	_____	○	_____
Train	_____		
Weather	_____		
Date	Wednesday		
		○	_____
		○	_____
Distance	_____	○	_____
Intensity	_____	○	_____
Cross-	_____	○	_____
Train	_____		
Weather	_____		
Date	Thursday		
		○	_____
		○	_____
Distance	_____	○	_____
Intensity	_____	○	_____
Cross-	_____	○	_____
Train	_____		
Weather	_____		
Date	Friday		
		○	_____
		○	_____
Distance	_____	○	_____
Intensity	_____	○	_____
Cross-	_____	○	_____
Train	_____		
Weather	_____		
Date	Saturday		
		○	_____
		○	_____
Distance	_____	○	_____
Intensity	_____	○	_____
Cross-	_____	○	_____
Train	_____		
Weather	_____		
Date	Sunday		
		○	_____
		○	_____
Distance	_____	○	_____
Intensity	_____	○	_____
Cross-	_____	○	_____
Train	_____		
Weather	_____		

Phase 4
Longer to Stronger

Intensity and Stamina

Weeks 26 - 30

Workout Weeks 26 – 30
Consolidation: Intensity and Stamina

<u>Notes:</u> Half Marathoners can go to the *Tapering* schedule after repeating the schedule below for two weeks.

Marathoners continue entire schedule.

Weeks 26 - 27:

Levels	Monday	Tuesday	Wednesday	Thursday	Friday	Saturday	Sunday
Beginner: Walk & jog (14-16 a/m/m)	Conditioning Exercises	Track w/o 1 mile of intervals	30 min. aerobic running	Tempo w/o 3 miles of tempo	c/t or rest	3 miles easy walk & jog	12 miles easy walk & jog
Intermediate: Jogger (11 – 13 a/m/m)	Conditioning Exercises	Track w/o 2 miles of intervals	45 min. aerobic running	Tempo w/o 6 miles of tempo	c/t or rest	3 miles easy jog	14 miles easy jog (last 4 miles tempo pace)
Advanced: Runner (7 – 10 a/m/m)	Conditioning Exercises	Track w/o 2.5 miles of intervals	60 min. aerobic running	Tempo w/o 8 miles of tempo	c/t or rest	5 miles easy jog	18 miles easy run (last 6 miles tempo pace)

Weeks 28 - 29:

Levels	Monday	Tuesday	Wednesday	Thursday	Friday	Saturday	Sunday
Beginner: Walk & jog (14-16 a/m/m)	Conditioning Exercises	Track w/o 1 mile of intervals	30 min. aerobic running	Tempo w/o 3 miles of tempo	c/t or rest	3 miles easy walk & jog	*12 -18 miles easy walk & jog
Intermediate: Runner (11 – 13 a/m/m)	Conditioning Exercises	Track w/o 2 miles of intervals	45 min. aerobic running	Tempo w/o 6 miles of tempo	c/t or rest	3 miles easy jog	15 – 22 miles easy jog (last 4 miles tempo pace)
Advanced: Runner (7 – 10 a/m/m)	Conditioning Exercises	Track w/o 2.5 miles of intervals	60 min. aerobic running	Tempo w/o 8 miles of tempo	c/t or rest	5 miles easy jog	20 - 24 miles easy run (last 6 miles tempo pace

Week 30:

Levels	Monday	Tuesday	Wednesday	Thursday	Friday	Saturday	Sunday
Beginner: Walk & jog (14-16 a/m/m)	Conditioning Exercises	Track w/o 1 mile of intervals	30 min. aerobic running	Tempo w/o 3 miles of tempo	c/t or rest	3 miles easy walk & jog	18 miles easy walk & jog
Intermediate: Runner (11 – 13 a/m/m)	Conditioning Exercises	Track w/o 2 miles of intervals	45 min. aerobic running	Tempo w/o 6 miles of tempo	c/t or rest	3 miles easy jog	22 miles easy jog (last 8 miles tempo pace)
Advanced: Runner (7 – 10 a/m/m)	Conditioning Exercises	Track w/o 2.5 miles of intervals	60 min. aerobic running	Tempo w/o 8 miles of tempo	c/t or rest	5 miles easy jog	24 miles easy run (last 12 miles tempo pace)

Week 26
Time for a Coach?

Why hire a running coach? What differentiates one running coach from another? A good coach is one who is professionally certified, has been in the sport of running for many years and experienced the many mental and physical aspects of both walkers and runners. A running coach can make the vision of the "finish line" into a reality for both the up and coming novice walker and the vintage runner. A coach will guide inexperienced runners to perform at their optimal physical, cardiovascular and mental level. Every sport has abundant learning curves such as form, technique, muscular necessities, agility requirements and many more factors which dictate success for the individual pursuing their full potential. The sport of distance walking or running is not exempt. A coach can help both walkers and runners stay motivated while guiding them with a gradual progression of miles to avoid injuries and not overwhelm them with a higher workload than their body is capable of. High performing runners require a coach to bring them to their highest potential, thus helping the participant reach his or her personal best in a given event.

So what kind of running coaches are we talking about? The kind of coach which will help you train SMARTER for a lifetime of fitness. Impact sports such as running do not allow for many form errors due to the repeated miles required in distance events. Both beginners and experienced runners now have countless opportunities which tempt them into doing a 5k, half marathon or marathon distance within a set amount of months. Experienced runners now expect improved time performances each year. Many will go through countless internet searches, books, and quick fixes and mixes of printed schedules in search of "the one" magic formula. A coach can cut through years of mixed training and give a more direct route to the finish line. Below are aspects of what can be expected by a certified walk to run coach for beginners, intermediate, and advanced levels.

SMARTER

S   Specific goal – The client presents their walk or run goal both in distance and time and a coach can provide a daily plan to progress toward that end. Inclusive are specific strength exercises and agility exercises which enhance forward movement and prevent injuries. A gradual daily schedule targets the time goal and progressively, yet gradually, develops duration so muscular adaptation takes place.

M   Measurable – The coach will require a benchmark of time per mile each month depending on one's aerobic ability; and will establish effort level pacing so an actual prediction of time can be forecast for the goal distance. Progress is largely measured by time taken for a given distance, perceived effort level, and actual accrued time per mile.

A   Attainable –The coach can be more objective in telling the client if the time and goal distant event is realistic given the time allotted for training. Aerobic capacity, correct form plus technique, and developed walking/running muscles are examples of a few key fitness markers which give the coach and client evidence of the attainability of the goal.

R   Relationship - The professional relationship between the coach and the client becomes increasingly advantageous since all forms of progress can be noted. The client has a sounding board to express training concerns such as injuries, breathing difficulties, race performances, etc. A coach can resolve those and other issues which come up. Most goal related training schedules last over three months such that physiological and cardiovascular improvements will necessitate a continual "tweaking" of training and conditioning workouts. The continuity established by having one coach will help greatly in making steadfast progress to reach the fitness goal desired.

T   Time – The time it takes to develop all energy, physical, and aerobic systems for an event distance goal will vary from client to client. The coach can contour a plan to fit the amount of days and time one has available to initiate and complete their workouts. Most running programs go in training phases and here again, the coach will assist and plan the timing of where each progressive training phase should begin and end.

E   Easy – Easy does it every time. Most participants if left to their own devices frequently leave out days and time of easy recovery running or walking. Fast walking and/or running day after day during a weekly cycle will create burnout and can result in overuse injuries. The coach will advise the client to not only put recovery such as slow jogging or walking into the workout, but will integrate recovery days with complimentary easy cross train days such as yoga, easy biking, or swimming. In each case the legs get a rest from impact and the participant comes back stronger and rested for the next training session. A special note for those over forty years old: the "easy" running or walking days should be around three per week since as we get older, recovery from the impact takes a bit longer.

R   Remain focused – There will be times during a fitness plan/schedule when the client may begin to miss workouts. The focus of the goal weakens and the participant may even stop the program or begin modifying the given plan. A coach will keep you motivated and have a remarkable influence on helping you stay with the plan. Running demands together with day to day life requirements can create increased mental stress on the body which may be already physically stressed. This is the time when the coach can modify your schedule and help bridge the "give in/give up" feeling, and put you on a more realistic plan which redirects your focus back to the fitness goal originally set.

There you have it. Training S M A R T E R goes a long way in providing success for individuals seeking long term and/or lifetime fitness goals. In sum, one does not have to go it alone and can become quite proficient in the sport of distance running or walking by being "coached" by a professional coach.

Week 27
Sharpen the Sword

Track training is the best bang for the buck in terms of increasing your VO2 max or aerobic capacity. The positive outcomes of both improved aerobic ability and leg economy come from a routine of weekly or bi-weekly track workouts. The tendency for those new to track is to go faster each week versus gaining a keen sense of pacing. Your job at a timed workout with set distances (repeats) is to develop consistent pacing while making your foot strike quicker and leg turnover faster. Also, the increased lung capacity gained will help you breathe more efficiently at slower speeds. Here are some basic explanations of what track workouts are all about. (See appendix 6 for level based track workouts)

Track Workout Defined: A series of short measured distances, or repeats while allowing rest for short intervals of time.

Purpose of Track Workouts: A weekly track workout increases overall speed, builds stamina, improves cardio vascular fitness, and improves leg economy. All these factors give the athlete tremendous running advantages in terms of becoming a faster and a more efficient runner.

Elements of a Track Workout:

1. Each track workout proceeds with at least a 5 minute easy jog or brisk walk and is followed by stretching each major muscle group.
2. A typical track workout is as follows:
   - 4-400 meters with intervals of 400 meters distance rest-walk/jog
   - 2-200 meters with intervals of 200 meters distance-walk/jog
   - 4-400 meters with intervals of 400 meters distance rest-walk/jog
3. Each track workout is followed with at least a 5 minute easy cool-down of either an easy jog or brisk walk.

Physiological Developments from track:

1. Measurable improvements in *cardiorespiratory fitness* – the health and function of the heart, lungs, and circulatory system. This occurs with both aerobic repeats and more so with anaerobic (without oxygen) fast running.
2. *Cardiorespiratory endurance increases* - the ability to sustain aerobic activity for prolonged periods
3. The capacity of the *lungs to exchange oxygen and carbon dioxide* with the blood; thus your *VO2 max* will improve.

4. The *circulatory system* works more efficiently in terms of transporting blood and nutrients to metabolically active tissues for longer periods of time.

5. A more *efficient heart rate* is established by practicing track workouts which are at 80% of maximum heart rate.

6. The *perceived exertion is reduced* on the easier paced runs due to a more efficient breathing rhythm and heart rate.

Week 28
Track – The Double Edge Sword

Too much of a good thing such as getting faster, can have some physiological consequences which must be respected. Running track repeats at 95% effort increases leg speed which then requires the Achilles tendon, calves, hamstrings, and various gluteus muscles to move up and down faster than they are accustomed to during day to day training. These muscle groups with their attached tendons and ligaments are contracting and getting tighter each time they are called upon to deliver faster speed. The buildup of lactic acid as your track workout proceeds makes your legs feel even heavier…yet you push on. Those are just a few reasons why many folks can pull muscles while engaging in a track session. How can we prevent the infamous "muscle pull" at track?

- *Warm up 5 minutes then stretch the major muscle groups.* This allows the muscles to lengthen and become more balanced.

- *Avoid going all out on the first or second repeat.* Gradually get up to 90%-95% effort speed. When you finish the repeats faster than you started that reveals good pacing as do consistent repeat times.

- *Avoid running track with someone who is faster.* Your competitive nature may force you to hyper extend muscle groups which may not be prepared to handle the new gait needed for faster movement.

- *Psychologically handle track as a way to increase leg turnover and VO2 max.* Avoid the pitfalls of going faster each week.

- *Have a coach look at your gait or get a gait analysis.* Many times the arms flare out, we hunch over a bit, and may not have an even landing pattern; all of which can create an injury due to overcompensation on one side of your body. Going fast will definitely magnify an incorrect gait.

- *After your track session, cool down 5 minutes* with an easy jog and or walk, and then gently stretch major muscle groups.

- *Put ice water on your legs within 15 minutes* after a vigorous track or tempo workout. Ice water will decrease inflammation immediately.

Week 29
The "Push" Advantage

Distance runners who desire to increase overall speed over the long distance are generally most successful when an even pace is learned and practiced as it relates to the time and distance goal. This is called "specificity of training" which is what a "push" achieves. Pushes are long distance stamina runs done for half to two thirds the distance of the goal length at 10-15 seconds quicker than the goal pace. For example if your goal is a 1:45 half marathon which is an 8:00 min pace, your "push" pace would be 7:50, and the longest "push" length would be 6-10 miles. Why are practicing "pushes" going to help secure your time goal?

- *The principle of specificity* is accomplished since your body is making adaptations with similar muscle groups, energy sources, and aerobic plus anaerobic energy sources which would be used during the goal event.

- *Practicing "overload" training forces your body to make specific adaptations* to be used during the actual event. Following an "overload" day such as a push with an "easy" day or rest or jogging will allow the muscles and tissues to rebuild and adapt to the stress of pushes.

- *The use of aerobic energy systems becomes more automatic as you practice pushing.* Initiating long distance pushes of a few miles results in an increased metabolic rate. Consequently the muscles now draw from the immediate source of fuel-glycogen as the faster running proceeds. After the glycogen stores are used up, fat will be the next fuel source. After two hours or more your energy source may actually be the protein enzymes from the muscles themselves. Protein can actually be considered an energy source for marathon runners.

- *"Pushes" help develop and call upon other energy systems.* To understand this, consider the order of the energy systems. The first energy source is glycogen which is stored in the muscles. As lactic acid is produced and released it is turned into another energy source called ATP (Adenosine Triphosphate). ATP can then be used as a fuel source by your running muscles when oxygen is present. Through the practice of "pushes", lactic acid develops then ATP allows you to build up a lactate tolerance which can move the glycogen around into the muscles giving more energy to run on. While gaining lactic acid and running through it, you have remaining fuel sources from both fat sources and muscles.

- *Establishing and simulating aerobic metabolism* is best accomplished through "pushes" since it requires the body to adapt, find, and use all your energy systems. Systematically as the "pushes" become longer so will the lactate threshold. Continuing bi-weekly pushes will teach the body to physiologically push through lactic acid build up or "the wall." Using this push training technique goes a long way to prevent this sluggish feeling before the race event ends.

Week 30
How to Race a Distance Event

When training vigorously and routinely many of us want to see improvements. Participating in a race event does just that. The camaraderie, the adrenaline of running a race, and the feeling you get from accomplishing your distance goal are but a few reasons why to take part in a race. Racing makes you mentally tough. Racing in mathematical terms for a 5K or 10K distance is a 90 to 95% effort as opposed to your easy jog which is 75% effort. Time goal half marathoners and marathoners generally go out about 80 – 85%% effort. In both cases, effort levels are more challenging than your normal training pace. The mental tenacity and physical execution of racing will benefit your training in many ways. First and foremost, mentally frame your "racing" experiences in an upbeat manner. A positive experience can be had if a few considerations are followed:

- *Eat carbohydrates an hour and a half before the event.* A plain bagel with a small amount of peanut butter, or an energy bar. In all cases make sure you have practiced eating the same pre-race "meal".

- *Drink water before, during, and after the race.* Put in a bit of Gatorade for the electrolytes, especially if the race day will be warm.

- *Keep the restroom nearby.* Generally go one more time 15 minutes before starting.

- *Get to the race early.* Figure out where the finish line is and starting line. Warm up about a half mile or a mile and get familiar with the course. If it is a half marathon or marathon, warm up less. Remember to stretch for 5-8 minutes after your warm up.

- *Plan a goal time.* Always have a plan A, B, and C; A-optimal, B-what you can live with, and C; finishing even though things went wrong along the way.

- *Finish with a kick.* Go hard those last 100 yards. You want to do your best, so finish with the fastest pace you can muster. Many races are won and competitors can be passed during the last 100 yards of a race.

- *Cool down when finished.* Don't collapse on the ground; slowly walk, hydrate, and then jog a half mile or so. Follow with easy stretching, and pour ice water on your legs to reduce inflammation.

- *Congratulate yourself and others.* Be proud of your accomplishment. Race performers make up less than a tenth of the population out there. By training and completing the race event you have demonstrated the act of doing your physical and mental best.

Everyone who got where he is had to begin where he was. Robert Lewis Stevenson

<u>**Week Beginning**</u>   /   /
Daily Schedule – Week 26
Miscellaneous Comments

Date	Monday		
Distance		○	
Intensity		○	
Cross-		○	
Train		○	
Weather		○	

Date	Tuesday		
Distance		○	
Intensity		○	
Cross-		○	
Train		○	
Weather		○	

Date	Wednesday		
Distance		○	
Intensity		○	
Cross-		○	
Train		○	
Weather		○	

Date	Thursday		
Distance		○	
Intensity		○	
Cross-		○	
Train		○	
Weather		○	

Date	Friday		
Distance		○	
Intensity		○	
Cross-		○	
Train		○	
Weather		○	

Date	Saturday		
Distance		○	
Intensity		○	
Cross-		○	
Train		○	
Weather		○	

Date	Sunday		
Distance		○	
Intensity		○	
Cross-		○	
Train		○	
Weather		○	

I love the challenge of starting at zero every day and seeing how much I can accomplish. Martha Stewart

<u>Week Beginning</u>   /   /

Daily Schedule – Week 27
Miscellaneous Comments

Date	Monday		
Distance Intensity Cross- Train Weather		○ ○ ○ ○ ○	_____ _____ _____ _____ _____
Date	Tuesday		
Distance Intensity Cross- Train Weather		○ ○ ○ ○ ○	_____ _____ _____ _____ _____
Date	Wednesday		
Distance Intensity Cross- Train Weather		○ ○ ○ ○ ○	_____ _____ _____ _____ _____
Date	Thursday		
Distance Intensity Cross- Train Weather		○ ○ ○ ○ ○	_____ _____ _____ _____ _____
Date	Friday		
Distance Intensity Cross- Train Weather		○ ○ ○ ○ ○	_____ _____ _____ _____ _____
Date	Saturday		
Distance Intensity Cross- Train Weather		○ ○ ○ ○ ○	_____ _____ _____ _____ _____
Date	Sunday		
Distance Intensity Cross- Train Weather		○ ○ ○ ○ ○	_____ _____ _____ _____ _____

I was not born strong, but I did know what I wanted and worked at it every day.
Theodore Roosevelt

Week Beginning / /
Daily Schedule – Week 28
Miscellaneous Comments

Date	Monday		
Distance Intensity Cross-Train Weather		○ ○ ○ ○ ○	_____
Date	Tuesday		
Distance Intensity Cross-Train Weather		○ ○ ○ ○ ○	_____
Date	Wednesday		
Distance Intensity Cross-Train Weather		○ ○ ○ ○ ○	_____
Date	Thursday		
Distance Intensity Cross-Train Weather		○ ○ ○ ○ ○	_____
Date	Friday		
Distance Intensity Cross-Train Weather		○ ○ ○ ○ ○	_____
Date	Saturday		
Distance Intensity Cross-Train Weather		○ ○ ○ ○ ○	_____
Date	Sunday		
Distance Intensity Cross-Train Weather		○ ○ ○ ○ ○	_____

I hate that feeling of going to bed at night when I don't feel like I pushed myself.
Steve Nash

Week Beginning / /
Daily Schedule – Week 29
Miscellaneous Comments

Date	Monday		
		○	_____
	_____	○	_____
Distance	_____	○	_____
Intensity	_____	○	_____
Cross-	_____	○	_____
Train	_____		
Weather	_____		
Date	Tuesday		
		○	_____
	_____	○	_____
Distance	_____	○	_____
Intensity	_____	○	_____
Cross-	_____	○	_____
Train	_____		
Weather	_____		
Date	Wednesday		
		○	_____
	_____	○	_____
Distance	_____	○	_____
Intensity	_____	○	_____
Cross-	_____	○	_____
Train	_____		
Weather	_____		
Date	Thursday		
		○	_____
	_____	○	_____
Distance	_____	○	_____
Intensity	_____	○	_____
Cross-	_____	○	_____
Train	_____		
Weather	_____		
Date	Friday		
		○	_____
	_____	○	_____
Distance	_____	○	_____
Intensity	_____	○	_____
Cross-	_____	○	_____
Train	_____		
Weather	_____		
Date	Saturday		
		○	_____
	_____	○	_____
Distance	_____	○	_____
Intensity	_____	○	_____
Cross-	_____	○	_____
Train	_____		
Weather	_____		
Date	Sunday		
		○	_____
	_____	○	_____
Distance	_____	○	_____
Intensity	_____	○	_____
Cross-	_____	○	_____
Train	_____		
Weather	_____		

When I was young, I was taught this doggerel: It's easy to be a starter, but are you a sticker too? It's easy enough to begin a job. It's harder to see it through.
Margaret Thatcher

<u>**Week Beginning**</u>   /   /
Daily Schedule – Week 30
Miscellaneous Comments

Date	Monday		○
Distance			○
Intensity			○
Cross-Train			○
Weather			○
Date	Tuesday		○
Distance			○
Intensity			○
Cross-Train			○
Weather			○
Date	Wednesday		○
Distance			○
Intensity			○
Cross-Train			○
Weather			○
Date	Thursday		○
Distance			○
Intensity			○
Cross-Train			○
Weather			○
Date	Friday		○
Distance			○
Intensity			○
Cross-Train			○
Weather			○
Date	Saturday		○
Distance			○
Intensity			○
Cross-Train			○
Weather			○
Date	Sunday		○
Distance			○
Intensity			○
Cross-Train			○
Weather			○

Phase 5
Rest to Race
The Taper

Weeks 31 - 33

Workout Weeks 31 - 33
Rest to Race – The Taper

<u>Notes:</u> Tapering indicates a period of time when mileage and intensity are reduced allowing for muscle recovery and mental rest.

Week 31:

Levels	Monday	Tuesday	Wednesday	Thursday	Friday	Saturday	Sunday
Beginner: Walk & jog (14-16 a/m/m)	Conditioning Exercises- the stretching component only	Track w/o 1/2 mile of intervals	30 min. easy walk & jog	2 miles of tempo	rest	3 miles easy walk & jog	10 miles easy walk & jog
Intermediate: Runner (11 – 13 a/m/m)	Conditioning Exercises- the stretching component only	Track w/o 1 mile of intervals	45 min. easy running	3 miles of tempo	rest	3 miles easy jog	13 miles easy jog (last 5 miles goal pace)
Advanced: Runner (7 – 10 a/m/m)	Conditioning Exercises- the stretching component only	Track w/o 1.5 miles of intervals	60 min. easy running	4 miles of tempo	rest	5 miles easy jog	15 miles easy run (last 5 miles goal pace)

Week 32:

Levels	Monday	Tuesday	Wednesday	Thursday	Friday	Saturday	Sunday
Beginner: Walk & jog (14-16 a/m/m)	Conditioning Exercises- the stretching component only	3 miles at race pace	30 min. easy walk and running	1 mile of tempo	rest	rest	8 miles easy walk & jog
Intermediate: Runner (11 – 13 a/m/m)	Conditioning Exercises- the stretching component only	4 miles at race pace	45 min. easy running	2 miles of tempo	rest	3 miles easy jog	10 miles easy jog (last 5 miles at goal pace)
Advanced: Runner (7 – 10 a/m/m)	Conditioning Exercises- the stretching component only	5 miles at race pace	60 min. easy running	3 miles of tempo	rest	5 miles easy jog	13 miles easy run (last 5 miles at goal pace)

Week 33:

Levels	Monday	Tuesday	Wednesday	Thursday	Friday	Saturday	Sunday
Beginner: Walk & jog (14-16 a/m/m)	Conditioning Exercises- the stretching component only	3 miles at race pace	30 min. easy walk and running	30 min. easy walk and running	rest	rest	Goal race!
Intermediate: Runner (11 – 13 a/m/m)	Conditioning Exercises- the stretching component only	4 miles at race pace	30 min. easy running	30 min. easy running	rest	rest	Goal race!
Advanced: Runner (7 – 10 a/m/m)	Conditioning Exercises- the stretching component only	5 miles at race pace	30 min. easy running	30 min. easy running	rest	rest	Goal race!

Week 31
Don't Lose Your Gains

All of this training has maximized your running speed, leg economy, endurance, and overall cardiovascular fitness. Tapering for a few weeks will serve to allow those athletic advantages to resurface during your goal distance event. Specifically what training should take place during the taper weeks?

Three weeks

- Keep the *VO2 maximum* by doing half the amount of repeats on the track. Complete a 5K run two to three weeks before as a confidence builder which will also tune up your maximum oxygen intake.
- Practice a *lactate threshold run* done just under goal pace. This second tune-up will keep the delayed lactate acid production response while running the goal event.
- Practice *one more long run* so your body is reminded how to use fat for fuel and so glycogen storage can be maintained as long as possible.

Two weeks

- Practice at a *5K race pace* on the track for 1.5 miles to sharpen leg turnover and retain cardiovascular gains.
- Take out your Monday run and replace it with short *100 yd. striders* mixed with a small amount of jogging
- Do one more 10K or 5K *time trial* at your planned half or whole marathon pace.
- Change from *aerobic running to jogging* on easy days.
- Eliminate *cross training* and one *extra day of running*.

One week

- Take out your *Monday* run.
- Practice your *goal race pace* on the track for the length of 3 - 5 miles.
- On the Thursday before, *jog for 30 minutes* or so and follow it with *2-4 striders*.
- Keep your *hydration practice* and *eating habits* the same. The quantity of food should not be excessive since extra weight can slow you down.
- *Get plenty of sleep*. Eliminate physical projects such as gardening and stressful events if at all possible.

Week 32
Race Psychology for Event Success

Training the mind is a large factor in long distance running events. Many participants say that 95% of the marathon challenge is pure mental toughness. Consider the length of time the mind must stay active, attentive to pace, and positive as inevitably challenges will occur before, during, and near the end. Half marathoners are a bit more confident of completing the distance; however the reality of holding a more vigorous pace brings upon its own challenge. Half marathoners also need to expect their final miles will bring on muscular fatigue. True of both distances, the mental aspects can be daunting. What are some mental preparations you can do to lessen the "demons" that come up during the actual running of your distance event?

- *Remember your training:* A well trained participant who has already done the distance and has the pace practiced routinely will have confidence of their physical ability and rate of speed.

- *Map out your run in segments:* Mentally go through various mileage segments and the pace you want to keep within each part. Take note of hills when establishing pacing since this will slow the steady pace down.

- *Lay out your three race day plans:* Here are three typical race day plans which can vary a bit from person to person. Plan A is a "no excuse" optimal weather day and when you feel physically fine. Plan B is considered when the weather is warmer than your training experiences, or the wind is strong, and/or the rain is coming down hard, plus you had little sleep. Plan C is implemented when it is "red flag" conditions; meaning too hot. Immediately hot conditions make us at risk for heat related illnesses, leg cramps, and early fatigue. Plan on just finishing as the goal. Plan C is definitely considered if you are going into the event injured.

- *Realize that there will be parts of the run that will be physically uncomfortable:* In practice make sure to take note of what mileage and pace your leg tiredness generally sets in. Then visualize running through it and finishing strong at the end.

- *Practice hydration stations:* Learn to anticipate how to grab the drink on the run or on the "jog." If you plan on walking each water station, figure out the amount of seconds you want to walk and make that time consistent.

- *Concentrate on your breathing and relax:* Each mile take a deep inhalation and remind the muscles to loosen up. Keep breathing steady and aerobic. Avoid breathing to hard at all costs unless it is right before the finish line.

- *Live in the "moment":* Enjoy the company and scenery while running, especially if it helps disassociate the physical and mental work through the more stressful miles.

- *Count to ten:* There can be testing issues which occur during the distance event. Most of them will not necessarily affect your performance unless you mentally allow it. We can usually handle ten "challenges" before going to Plan B or C. Some challenging ones you may face are: increment weather, lack of sleep, falling down, chafing, blisters, headphones not working, untied shoelace, forgetting gloves, and the list goes on. Note: In most cases hot weather, over 80 degrees does necessitate going to plan C.

Week 33
Week to the Day!

By now you are in place to walk, run, or race the event. The idea of going hard and long this week is not going to change your race day performance, but hinder it. The body needs to physically rest and restore all fuel systems to their "full" point. Mentally the time of rest may make you anxious since there will be little if any energy expended before the goal event. Learn to live with it for this week. Your glycogen storage must get optimally full, your muscles need to rest and heal, and your mental set must be calmed. What are the "rules" of race week? How does one begin their goal event?

- *Do not change your diet in terms of types of food.* Lower mileage will make you less hungry so the quantity of food may lessen. Continue your diet of carbohydrate rich foods.

- *Do not take new supplements or medicines during this week.* Keep taking the same hydration replacement drink and foods which you used in training.

- *Don't replace all your new energy with big physical projects.* Avoid room renovation or landscaping your lawn. All your physical energy should be conserved.

- *Sleep earlier during that week…* or at least, settle down earlier each evening.

- *Arrive at the half marathon or marathon expo with the idea of picking up your packet vs. standing on your feet for hours shopping.* All the energy you expend the day before will subtract from your performance the day of; especially in a marathon.

- *The night before, layout all clothing, attach the race number, your chip, and get your food replacements ready, etc.* Check out the weather one more time for inclement weather conditions and wear clothes which support those conditions. Be prepared to throw away some layers as you proceed through the early miles.

- *You may not sleep soundly the evening before.* That is a common experience among distance event participants. It is the week of and two nights before the event which a full nights' sleep becomes important. Avoid sleeping aids since this can alter the pace and your mental toughness.

- *Watch an inspiring running movie or read a good book which lifts your spirits the evening before.* This will help you mentally make positive affirmations on race day.

- *Eat a simple carbohydrate breakfast an hour and a half before.* Do not try anything you haven't eaten during your practice sessions.

- *Arrive at the race early.* This will prevent your nerves from getting out of control. Hydrate as usual and stop drinking a half hour before the race. Stop at the restroom 15 minutes before the start just in case.

- *For the first mile or two, begin the race slower than race pace.* Gradually go to race pace. Any deviation from that statement will most likely result in a sluggish last few miles in the half and possibly more in the whole. When you are well trained, the time lost in the beginning will be made up at the end and then some.

Week 34
The Next Step

Congratulations! You completed your long distance event. The feelings of accomplishment and joy are all yours to share with those around you. Plus the physical empowerment of completing such a challenging goal as a half or whole have put you into a complete new physical arena. You are now fitter than when the journey first began. After such an accomplishment the mind quickly begins a frantic search of what to do next. How does one experience that thrill over again? What happens now to all the new friends and experiences shared along the fitness way?

Let's back up a bit and go through some steps to begin immediately after going through the finish line. Each of these will help the body recover more quickly.

Finish line

* Drink plenty of *water* and *electrolyte* replacement within 15 minutes finishing. You may not realize it but the body is dehydrated and is in definite need of hydration and salt replacement.

* Within an hour take a *protein and carbohydrate* combination food or liquid. This could range from yogurt, fruit shakes, ice cream; all of which are usually in the food area at the event.

* *Walk* as much as possible after finishing; especially a marathon. The walk will stretch out the muscles, gradually lower the heart rate and core temperature. The brief walk will also prevent muscle spasms and general muscle tightness. After a brief walk and some standing up stretching (no sitting down), ice massage the legs fully.

Evening of race

* The *ice bath* after a long distance run will quickly reduce muscle inflammation and establish a quicker recovery rate. No sauna or hot tubs now; either of those will increase inflammation.

* Continue drinking lots of *water* throughout the day to rid the lactic acid and waste products produced while running. Eat *protein rich foods* since the muscles used lots of protein to carry you all the way to the finish line.

Post week

* Get a *massage* after three days and make sure it is a recovery massage. A gentle yoga class is highly recommended.

* *Walk to run* with the idea of stretching after each mile or earlier. Do this every other day and cross-train lightly with swimming or biking; again at an easy effort pace.

The Next Step

You took good care of yourself physically during the first week of your post-race. Now, what is next? Most of us are ready to get started on new fitness adventures and want to continue staying fit. Even if the goal is to take it easy for one month; so be it. Consider these future goals:

* If a half marathon, now is the time to think of training for a whole marathon.

* For both the half or whole, one may now want to set a goal to go faster.

* Many folks like to make future events a destination run and travel to the site; most likely with some friends.

* Some marathoners look into doing the fifty states; a marathon in each state. Whoops...you have to get 10 states done before you join this club.

* There are those who want to go for ultra-distance. The marathon was rewarding but what about something like multiple weekend races; first a half, then a whole all in one weekend!

This list of ideas is exciting and necessitates continued fitness. Fitness goals are only limited by one's imagination. Between reading and seeing other events all over the world and hearing tempting ideas from friends, you will never "run" out of steps!

The big secret in life is that there is no big secret. Whatever your goal, you can get there if you are willing to work. Oprah Winfrey

<u>**Week Beginning**</u>   /   /
Daily Schedule – Week 31
Miscellaneous Comments

Date	Monday		
Distance		○	___
Intensity		○	___
Cross-Train		○	___
Weather		○	___
		○	___

Date	Tuesday		
Distance		○	___
Intensity		○	___
Cross-Train		○	___
Weather		○	___
		○	___

Date	Wednesday		
Distance		○	___
Intensity		○	___
Cross-Train		○	___
Weather		○	___
		○	___

Date	Thursday		
Distance		○	___
Intensity		○	___
Cross-Train		○	___
Weather		○	___
		○	___

Date	Friday		
Distance		○	___
Intensity		○	___
Cross-Train		○	___
Weather		○	___
		○	___

Date	Saturday		
Distance		○	___
Intensity		○	___
Cross-Train		○	___
Weather		○	___
		○	___

Date	Sunday		
Distance		○	___
Intensity		○	___
Cross-Train		○	___
Weather		○	___
		○	___

A truly happy person is someone who never quite reaches the rainbow's end. Mary Kay Ash

**Week Beginning   /   /   **
Daily Schedule – Week 32
Miscellaneous Comments

Date	Monday		
Distance Intensity Cross-Train Weather		○ ○ ○ ○ ○	
Date	**Tuesday**		
Distance Intensity Cross-Train Weather		○ ○ ○ ○ ○	
Date	**Wednesday**		
Distance Intensity Cross-Train Weather		○ ○ ○ ○ ○	
Date	**Thursday**		
Distance Intensity Cross-Train Weather		○ ○ ○ ○ ○	
Date	**Friday**		
Distance Intensity Cross-Train Weather		○ ○ ○ ○ ○	
Date	**Saturday**		
Distance Intensity Cross-Train Weather		○ ○ ○ ○ ○	
Date	**Sunday**		
Distance Intensity Cross-Train Weather		○ ○ ○ ○ ○	

You've got to work at living….99 and 9/10 percent of Americans work on dying! You've got to eat right, exercise, and have goals and challenges. Exercise is king; nutrition is queen. Put them together and you've got a kingdom. Jack LaLanne at age 90

Week Beginning   /   /
Daily Schedule – Week 33
Miscellaneous Comments

Date	Monday		
_____	_____	○	_____
Distance	_____	○	_____
Intensity	_____	○	_____
Cross-	_____	○	_____
Train	_____	○	_____
Weather			
Date	**Tuesday**		
_____	_____	○	_____
Distance	_____	○	_____
Intensity	_____	○	_____
Cross-	_____	○	_____
Train	_____	○	_____
Weather			
Date	**Wednesday**		
_____	_____	○	_____
Distance	_____	○	_____
Intensity	_____	○	_____
Cross-	_____	○	_____
Train	_____	○	_____
Weather			
Date	**Thursday**		
_____	_____	○	_____
Distance	_____	○	_____
Intensity	_____	○	_____
Cross-	_____	○	_____
Train	_____	○	_____
Weather			
Date	**Friday**		
_____	_____	○	_____
Distance	_____	○	_____
Intensity	_____	○	_____
Cross-	_____	○	_____
Train	_____	○	_____
Weather			
Date	**Saturday**		
_____	_____	○	_____
Distance	_____	○	_____
Intensity	_____	○	_____
Cross-	_____	○	_____
Train	_____	○	_____
Weather			
Date	**Sunday**		
_____	_____	○	_____
Distance	_____	○	_____
Intensity	_____	○	_____
Cross-	_____	○	_____
Train	_____	○	_____
Weather			

True of running, true of walking, true of life...always move forward. Lynn Gray

Week Beginning _____ / _____ / _____
Daily Schedule – Week 34
Miscellaneous Comments

Date	Monday		
Distance Intensity Cross-Train Weather		○ ○ ○ ○ ○	_____ _____ _____ _____ _____
Date	Tuesday		
Distance Intensity Cross-Train Weather		○ ○ ○ ○ ○	_____ _____ _____ _____ _____
Date	Wednesday		
Distance Intensity Cross-Train Weather		○ ○ ○ ○ ○	_____ _____ _____ _____ _____
Date	Thursday		
Distance Intensity Cross-Train Weather		○ ○ ○ ○ ○	_____ _____ _____ _____ _____
Date	Friday		
Distance Intensity Cross-Train Weather		○ ○ ○ ○ ○	_____ _____ _____ _____ _____
Date	Saturday		
Distance Intensity Cross-Train Weather		○ ○ ○ ○ ○	_____ _____ _____ _____ _____
Date	Sunday		
Distance Intensity Cross-Train Weather		○ ○ ○ ○ ○	_____ _____ _____ _____ _____

Appendix #1

Key Race/Time Trial Results – put into logbook

Event name	Date	Phase	Time Goal/Actual Time	Experience

1. _____

2. _____

3. _____

4. _____

5. _____

6. _____

7. _____

8. _____

9. _____

10. _____

11. _____

12. _____

13. _____

14. _____

15. _____

16. _____

17. _____

18. _____

19. _____

20. _____

21. _____

22. _____

23. _____

24. _____

25. _____

Appendix #2
Walk to Run Terms

Aerobic: any exercise which allows adequate oxygen to be delivered into the cells to meet the energy output required such as in: running, swimming, and biking.

Anaerobic: an effort where breathing is next to impossible due to faster than normal physical exertion and lung capacity reaching its' maximum capacity.

ATP: the body's energy source known as adenosine triphosphate generally produced by faster running. The quicker the cell produces ATP the more the cell can function before it fatigues. Aerobic and anaerobic training both help muscle cells replenish the amount of ATP stored.

Bounding: a pronounced leg lift while moving slightly forward.

Cardiorespiratory fitness: the capacity of the lungs to exchange oxygen and carbon dioxide with the blood and the circulatory system's ability to transport blood and nutrients to metabolically active tissues for sustained periods of time without total fatigue.

Cardiorespiratory endurance: having the ability to sustain aerobic activity for a prolonged period of time.

Cardiovascular fitness: the capability of the heart, organs and lungs to consume, transport, and utilize oxygen.

Core: refers to one's stomach and chest; a strong core becomes critical in all sports since it provides balance and adds coordination to both arms and legs.

Duration: the amount of time engaged in during your aerobic workout.

Effort based running: Running based on effort range refers to the perceived personal effort put forth when there is not a pre-determined distance or set time goal to meet. It is common to walk or run at a "medium effort" meaning 80-85% of your heart rate during a half marathon, or a "hard effort" meaning 85%-90% of your heart rate during a 5K.

Endurance: the amount of time and/or distance you can sustain at a given aerobic effort without total muscle fatigue.

Frequency: the amount of times per week and/or per day engaged in during your aerobic workout.

Interval: a given amount of time and/or distance for recovery between repeats on a track.

Heart rate: the number of times the heart beats per minute(bpm) which can be determined by taking the resting pulse rate for 30 seconds and multiplying that number by two.

Hypernatremia: too much water taken in while walking or running results in this electrolyte imbalance; resulting in nausea, dizziness, and sometimes death.

Intensity: the addition of resistance while engaged in during your aerobic activity; track is an example because of the increased speed required.

Jog: a slow movement of running which accommodates recovery; usually done at a 70-75% perceived effort rate. Jogging is also a term frequently used by beginner runners learning to go slow while building distance.

Law of specificity: An individual can become both functional and efficient of any given movement, as long as the movement is trained and practiced over and over again. For example, high leg lifting for hill runs can be specifically trained for by a regiment of leg lifts with an ankle weight.

Lactic acid: is a by-product of ATP production and results in an increase of lactic acid which then limits the contraction and functioning of muscular movement. A common example occurs during a track workout when ATP production occurs resulting in lactic acid build up.

Leg turnover: refers to the ability to run quickly by increasing the speed of your legs moving up and down; leg turnover is generally determined and limited by coordination and aerobic capacity.

Negative splits: a given distance such as a mile, which can be repeated a bit faster each time; the preferred way of finishing your distance goal event.

Overpronation: generally caused by having flat feet or high arches – which results in a pronounced inward foot roll or a marked outward foot roll.

Personal Record: also known by the acronym of running a PR A personal record or personal best is a lower time barrier made on a given goal distance.

Push: the execution of continuous miles just below goal pace; usually done on a progressive bi-weekly basis.

Pronation: the normal sequence of a foot strike is to land slightly on the heel then rolling slightly inward as it centers itself for balance; these movements regulate an equal distribution of foot impact.

Race Pace: the pace one can sustain both physically and aerobically during the entire distance of the goal distance event.

Repeats: a track related term meaning a specific distance on the track will be repeated and timed; top objectives include challenging the aerobic system plus increasing leg turnover.

Resistance: adding additional stress to legs while running; examples include: uphill running, striders or 100 yd. dashes on tired legs, or running after biking.

Resting heart rate: is measured most accurately just before getting out of bed and can be found on the larger carotid artery on the side of the larynx or by the pulse on the wrist - an ideal fitness marker would be in the mid-forties to low fifties.

Specificity of Movement: An individual can become both functional and efficient of any given movement, as long as that movement is repeated over and over again. Running a marathon for example is most successfully done when long distance runs are practiced.

Stamina: holding a medium to hard effort for a distance which puts you at a perceived effort range of 80 – 90%.

Striders: running approximately 100 yds with the following progression: first 25 yds. At an easy effort for form, next 25 yds. do at a medium effort, last 25 yds. run all out at a 95% effort.

Supination: is caused by a high arch causing much of your weight to fall toward the outside of the foot. This continual foot strike can lead to iliotibial band tightness around the knee.

Taper: a term referred to when the distance walker or runner cuts down mileage and intensity prior to their goal distance event.

Tempo: short speed bursts run a bit faster than the aerobic pace or at 80 – 85% of your perceived effort range.

Time Trial: a simulated race effort done informally to obtain feedback of your current cardiorespiratory fitness and general physical condition.

VO2 Max: the maximum volume of oxygen your body can consume and use.

Workout: refers to the actual length, time, and effort for each distance given.

WEIGHTS

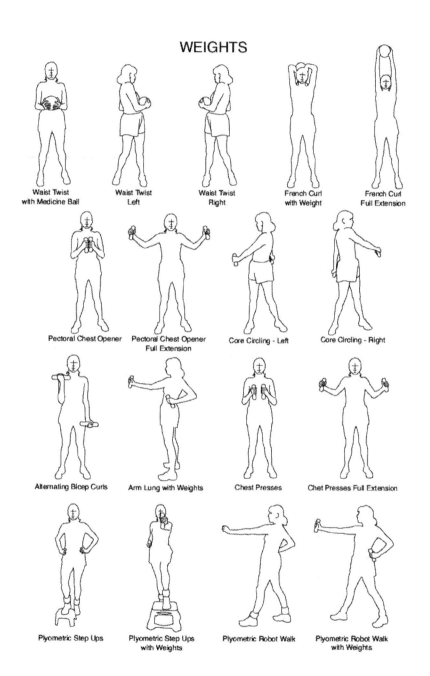

Waist Twist with Medicine Ball

Waist Twist Left

Waist Twist Right

French Curl with Weight

French Curl Full Extension

Pectoral Chest Opener

Pectoral Chest Opener Full Extension

Core Circling - Left

Core Circling - Right

Alternating Bicep Curls

Arm Lung with Weights

Chest Presses

Chet Presses Full Extension

Plyometric Step Ups

Plyometric Step Ups with Weights

Plyometric Robot Walk

Plyometric Robot Walk with Weights

STRETCHES

Butterfly Stretch

Wedge Calf Strech
Toes Forward

Wedge Calf Strech
Toes Out

Wedge Calf Strech
Toes In

Core Circling - Left

Core Circling - Right

Spinal Twist Left

Spinal Twist Right

Toe Raises

Sit Down Hip Flexor
Stretch

Hamstring Stretch with Rope

Quad-Thigh Stretch

Plank

Abdominal Curl - Front

Abdominal Curl - Left Oblique

Abdominal Curl - Right Oblique

Appendix #5
Food Journal

Weekly Template

Day: _____

Time of Day	Food and amount eaten	Activity for the day

Appendix #6
Fifty Track and Tempo Workouts

Ability Level Based: BL = Beginner Level, IL = Intermediate Level, A = Advanced Level

Workout level & emphasis	*Distance	Track Interval workout-r/p 90% effort	Tempo or "push" workout 80 % effort
#1 – BL Leg turnover and leg speed	1-2 miles	8 x 200 Walk 200 during intervals	8 x 200 Jog 200 during intervals
#2 – BL Leg turnover and leg speed	1-2 miles	12 x 200, Walk 200 during intervals	12 x 200 Jog 200 during intervals
#3 – BL Leg turnover and leg speed	1-2 miles	6 x 400 Walk 200 during intervals	6 x 400 Jog 400 during intervals
#4 – BL Leg turnover and leg speed	2 miles	8 x 400 Walk 200 during intervals	8 x 400 Jog 400 during intervals
#5 – BL Leg turnover & stamina	2 miles	4 x 400, 2 x 200 jog 200 during intervals	4 x 400, 8x 200, Jog 400 during intervals

Workout level & emphasis	*Distance	Track Interval workout-r/p 90% effort	Tempo or "push" workout 80 % effort
#6 – BL Leg turnover & resistance	1-2 miles	8 x 200 uphill Walk downhill	8 x 200 Jog 200 downhill
#7 – BL Leg turnover & resistance	1-2 miles	8 x 400 uphill Walk downhill	8 x 400 uphill Jog 400 downhill
#8 – BL Leg turnover & resistance	1-2 miles	2 x 800 uphill Jog downhill	4 x 800 uphill Jog downhill
#9 – BL Leg turnover & resistance	1-2 miles	3 x 800 uphill Jog downhill	6 x 800 uphill Jog downhill
#10-BL Run even splits	2-3 miles	10 x 400 Walk 100 during intervals	12 x 400 Jog during intervals

Workout level & emphasis	*Distance	Track Interval workout-r/p 90% effort	Tempo or "push" workout 80 % effort
#11-IL Run negative splits	2-3 miles	10 x 400, 1 second faster each one Walk 100 during intervals	12 x 400, 1 second faster each one Walk 100 during intervals
#12-IL Equal effort running	2-3 miles	10 x 400, equal effort Jog 400 during each interval	10 x 2 minutes, equal effort, jog 2 min between each tempo
#13-IL Run negative splits	2-3 miles	10 x 400, 1 second faster each one Jog 400 during each interval	10 x uphill, 1 second faster each time on same hill, 2 min recovery
#14-BL Long distance stamina	2-3 miles	4 x 800 Walk 4 minutes during intervals	4 x 800, jog 5 minutes between each tempo
#15-BL Long distance stamina	2-3 miles	1 x 1 mile, 2 x 800, walk 4 minutes during intervals	1 x 1 mile, jog 5 minutes, 2 x 5 min., jog 5 min. between each tempo

Workout level & emphasis	*Distance	Track Interval workout-r/p 90% effort	Tempo or "push" workout 80 % effort
#16-IL Long distance stamina	2-3 miles	6 x 800, jog 400 during intervals	6 x 5 min., jog 3 min. between each 6 min. tempo
#17-IL Run negative splits	2-3 miles	6 x 800, 3 seconds faster each one, jog 400 during intervals	6 x 6 min., jog 6 min. between each 6 min. tempo, last one repeat go race pace
#18-IL Long distance stamina	3 miles	2 x 1200, 2 x 800, walk 200 during intervals	2 x 10 min, 2 x 5 min, jog 5 min between each tempo time
#19-IL Long distance stamina	3 miles	2 x 1200, 2 x 800, jog 400 during intervals	3 x 10 min, jog 5 min between each tempo time
#20-IL Stamina and leg turnover	2-3 miles	1-1200, 4 x 400, 1-1200, jog 200 during intervals	2 x 10 min, 5 x 3 min, jog 3 min between each tempo time
#21-IL Leg turnover and leg speed	2-3 miles	15 x 200, jog 200 during intervals	10 x 3 min, jog 3 min between each tempo time

Workout level & emphasis	*Distance	Track Interval workout-r/p 90% effort	Tempo or "push" workout 80 % effort
#27-IL Long distance stamina w/resistance	3 miles	3 x 1 mile with 4-5 min rest between, follow with 5-100 yd striders	3 x 1 mile with 5 min job in between, follow with 5-100 yd. striders, or 5 uphill repeats, recover on way down
#28-IL Finish strong	3 miles	2 x 800, 4 x 400, 2 x 800 with 200 jog for each interval	2 x 4 min., 8 x 2 min, 2 x 4 min, with 3 min. jog in between
#29-IL Learn 5K race pace	3 miles	12 x 400, rest 1 min. for each interval, keep repeats the same time	8 x ½ mile at just below desired race pace, rest 3 min during each interval
#30-IL Learn 5K race pace	3 miles	3 x 1 mile with 30 sec. rest between each mile	5K time trial at desired goal race pace
#31-IL Increase leg turnover & leg efficiency	3+ miles	8 x 200 with 30 sec rest interval, 8 x 400 with 1 min. rest interval	15 x 2 min tempo pace with 2 min jog each interval

Workout level & emphasis	*Distance	Track Interval workout-r/p 90% effort	Tempo or "push" workout 80 % effort
#27-IL Long distance stamina w/resistance	3 miles	3 x 1 mile with 4-5 min rest between, follow with 5-100 yd striders	3 x 1 mile with 5 min job in between, follow with 5-100 yd. striders, or 5 uphill repeats, recover on way down
#28-IL Finish strong	3 miles	2 x 800, 4 x 400, 2 x 800 with 200 jog for each interval	2 x 4 min., 8 x 2 min, 2 x 4 min, with 3 min. jog in between
#29-IL Learn 5K race pace	3 miles	12 x 400, rest 1 min. for each interval, keep repeats the same time	8 x ½ mile at just below desired race pace, rest 3 min during each interval
#30-IL Learn 5K race pace	3 miles	3 x 1 mile with 30 sec. rest between each mile	5K time trial at desired goal race pace
#31-IL Increase leg turnover & leg efficiency	3+ miles	8 x 200 with 30 sec rest interval, 8 x 400 with 1 min. rest interval	15 x 2 min tempo pace with 2 min jog each interval

Workout level & emphasis	*Distance	Track Interval workout-r/p 90% effort	Tempo or "push" workout 80 % effort
#32-IL Increase aerobic threshold	3 miles	8 sets of: 1-400, jog 200, 1-400 with 3 min. rest interval	6 sets of: ¼ mile, jog 2 min., ¼, repeat process 6 times, with 5 min jog between
#33-IL Yasso© workout	3 miles	6 – 800s at your predicted marathon or half marathon pace	8 x 5 min. of tempo, with 5 min jog each interval
#34-IL Pre-race mid-week warm-up for key race	3 miles	5 striders, 5 – 200s, 5-400s, 5-200s, 5striders-1 min. recovery during intervals	10 x ¼ mile uphill, jog downhill
35-IL Time trial to determine your aerobic ability	3.1 miles	5K run on measured course, or track if necessary	6 miles at a pace 5-10 seconds below desired goal race pace. Stop after 3 miles for water (30 seconds).

Workout level & emphasis	*Distance	Track Interval workout-r/p 90% effort	Tempo or "push" workout 80 % effort
36-A Increase aerobic endurance and leg speed	4 miles	8 x 400, jog 1 mile, 8 x 400	8 x ¾ mile with 3 min. jog in each interval
37-A Increase leg turnover and leg speed	4 miles	12 x 400, with 200 jog during intervals	4 continuous miles, jog 1 mile, 2 miles at 5K race speed
38-A Increase leg speed and anaerobic threshold	4 miles	20 x 200 with 100 yd jog during intervals	6 continuous miles, with 6 x 2 min. speed bursts at 5K race pace
39-A Increase speed endurance	4 miles	16 x 400, with 200 yd. jog during interval	10 x 3 min race pace, with ½ mile tempo between each 3 min.
40-A Increase stamina	4-5 miles	12-15 x 400 with a 2 min rest during intervals	10K at tempo pace, followed by 6 x 2 min. race pace, with 30 sec. rest during intervals
41-A Increase stamina and leg speed	4-5 miles	20 x 200, with 1 min. rest during intervals	8 continuous miles at 5 seconds below desired long distance goal race pace

Workout level & emphasis	*Distance	Track Interval workout-r/p 90% effort	Tempo or "push" workout 80 % effort
42-A Yasso workout	5 miles	10 x 800 at your predicted marathon or half marathon pace	10-12 continuous miles, run 5 seconds below desired goal race pace
43-A Increase leg speed and endurance	5 miles	20 x 400 with 400 jog during each interval	20 x 5 min. with 5 min jog during each interval
44-A Finish strong on tired legs	5 miles	15 x 400 with 200 jog during each interval, reduce each lap by 1-2 seconds	6 continuous miles, then 10 ¼ mile hill repeats, jog downhill for recovery
45-A Predict goal race time	6 miles	10K at 5K race pace	12 continuous miles, run 5 seconds below desired long distance goal race pace
46-A Increase leg speed-stamina	6 miles	24 x 200, with 2 min. rest during intervals	10 continuous miles, with 10 x 1 min. race pace spurts along the way
48-A Increase endurance	6 miles	3 x 2 mile with 400 jog during each interval	6 x 2 mile with 5 min. jog during each interval

Workout level & emphasis	*Distance	Track Interval workout-r/p 90% effort	Tempo or "push" workout 80 % effort
49-A Increase leg speed	5 miles	5 x 1 mile with 2 min. rest during each interval	10 x 1 mile, with 5 min. jog during each interval
50-A Increase stamina & endurance	6 miles	10 x 200, 8 x 400, 6 x 800	10 continuous miles followed with 8-10 ¼ mile hill repeats, jog downhill for recovery

Appendix 7

PACING CHART

1 M	5K	10K	15K	20K	1/2 Marathon 21.1K	25K	30K	Marathon 42.2K
0:05:00	0:15:32	0:31:05	0:46:37	1:02:09	1:05:30	1:18:08	1:33:14	2:11:06
0:05:05	0:15:48	0:31:36	0:47:23	1:03:11	1:06:36	1:19:26	1:34:47	2:13:17
0:05:10	0:16:03	0:32:07	0:48:10	1:04:13	1:07:41	1:20:44	1:36:20	2:15:28
0:05:15	0:16:19	0:32:38	0:48:57	1:05:15	1:08:47	1:22:02	1:37:53	2:17:39
0:05:20	0:16:34	0:33:09	0:49:43	1:06:18	1:09:52	1:23:20	1:39:26	2:19:50
0:05:25	0:16:50	0:33:40	0:50:30	1:07:20	1:10:58	1:24:38	1:41:00	2:22:02
0:05:30	0:17:05	0:34:11	0:51:16	1:08:22	1:12:03	1:25:56	1:42:33	2:24:13
0:05:35	0:17:21	0:34:42	0:52:03	1:09:24	1:13:09	1:27:14	1:44:06	2:26:24
0:05:40	0:17:37	0:35:13	0:52:50	1:10:26	1:14:14	1:28:33	1:45:39	2:28:35
0:05:45	0:17:52	0:35:44	0:53:36	1:11:28	1:15:20	1:29:51	1:47:13	2:30:46
0:05:50	0:18:08	0:36:15	0:54:23	1:12:31	1:16:25	1:31:09	1:48:46	2:32:57
0:05:55	0:18:23	0:36:46	0:55:10	1:13:33	1:17:31	1:32:27	1:50:19	2:35:08
0:06:00	0:18:39	0:37:17	0:55:56	1:14:35	1:18:36	1:33:45	1:51:52	2:37:19
0:06:05	0:18:54	0:37:48	0:56:43	1:15:37	1:19:42	1:35:03	1:53:25	2:39:30
0:06:10	0:19:10	0:38:20	0:57:29	1:16:39	1:20:47	1:36:21	1:54:59	2:41:41
0:06:15	0:19:25	0:38:51	0:58:16	1:17:41	1:21:53	1:37:39	1:56:32	2:43:53
0:06:20	0:19:41	0:39:22	0:59:03	1:18:43	1:22:58	1:38:58	1:58:05	2:46:04
0:06:25	0:19:56	0:39:53	0:59:49	1:19:46	1:24:04	1:40:16	1:59:38	2:48:15
0:06:30	0:20:12	0:40:24	1:00:36	1:20:48	1:25:09	1:41:34	2:01:12	2:50:26
0:06:35	0:20:27	0:40:55	1:01:22	1:21:50	1:26:15	1:42:52	2:02:45	2:52:37
0:06:40	0:20:43	0:41:26	1:02:09	1:22:52	1:27:20	1:44:10	2:04:18	2:54:48
0:06:45	0:20:59	0:41:57	1:02:56	1:23:54	1:28:26	1:45:28	2:05:51	2:56:59
0:06:50	0:21:14	0:42:28	1:03:42	1:24:56	1:29:31	1:46:46	2:07:24	2:59:10
0:06:55	0:21:30	0:42:59	1:04:29	1:25:58	1:30:37	1:48:04	2:08:58	3:01:21
0:07:00	0:21:45	0:43:30	1:05:15	1:27:01	1:31:42	1:49:23	2:10:31	3:03:32
0:07:05	0:22:01	0:44:01	1:06:02	1:28:03	1:32:48	1:50:41	2:12:04	3:05:44
0:07:10	0:22:16	0:44:32	1:06:49	1:29:05	1:33:53	1:51:59	2:13:37	3:07:55
0:07:15	0:22:32	0:45:04	1:07:35	1:30:07	1:34:59	1:53:17	2:15:11	3:10:06
0:07:20	0:22:47	0:45:35	1:08:22	1:31:09	1:36:04	1:54:35	2:16:44	3:12:17
0:07:25	0:23:03	0:46:06	1:09:09	1:32:11	1:37:10	1:55:53	2:18:17	3:14:28
0:07:30	0:23:18	0:46:37	1:09:55	1:33:14	1:38:15	1:57:11	2:19:50	3:16:39
0:07:35	0:23:34	0:47:08	1:10:42	1:34:16	1:39:21	1:58:29	2:21:24	3:18:50
0:07:40	0:23:49	0:47:39	1:11:28	1:35:18	1:40:26	1:59:48	2:22:57	3:21:01
0:07:45	0:24:05	0:48:10	1:12:15	1:36:20	1:41:32	2:01:06	2:24:30	3:23:12
0:07:50	0:24:21	0:48:41	1:13:02	1:37:22	1:42:37	2:02:24	2:26:03	3:25:23
0:07:55	0:24:36	0:49:12	1:13:48	1:38:24	1:43:43	2:03:42	2:27:36	3:27:35
0:08:00	0:24:52	0:49:43	1:14:35	1:39:26	1:44:48	2:05:00	2:29:10	3:29:46
0:08:05	0:25:07	0:50:14	1:15:21	1:40:29	1:45:54	2:06:18	2:30:43	3:31:57
0:08:10	0:25:23	0:50:45	1:16:08	1:41:31	1:46:59	2:07:36	2:32:16	3:34:08
0:08:15	0:25:38	0:51:16	1:16:55	1:42:33	1:48:05	2:08:54	2:33:49	3:36:19
0:08:20	0:25:54	0:51:48	1:17:41	1:43:35	1:49:10	2:10:13	2:35:23	3:38:30
0:08:25	0:26:09	0:52:19	1:18:28	1:44:37	1:50:16	2:11:31	2:36:56	3:40:41
0:08:30	0:26:25	0:52:50	1:19:15	1:45:39	1:51:21	2:12:49	2:38:29	3:42:52
0:08:35	0:26:40	0:53:21	1:20:01	1:46:41	1:52:27	2:14:07	2:40:02	3:45:03
0:08:40	0:26:56	0:53:52	1:20:48	1:47:44	1:53:32	2:15:25	2:41:35	3:47:14
0:08:45	0:27:11	0:54:23	1:21:34	1:48:46	1:54:38	2:16:43	2:43:09	3:49:26
0:08:50	0:27:27	0:54:54	1:22:21	1:49:48	1:55:43	2:18:01	2:44:42	3:51:37
0:08:55	0:27:43	0:55:25	1:23:08	1:50:50	1:56:49	2:19:19	2:46:15	3:53:48
0:09:00	0:27:58	0:55:56	1:23:54	1:51:52	1:57:54	2:20:38	2:47:48	3:55:59

1M	2 M	3 M	4 M	5 M	10 M	1/2 Marathon 13.1 M	15 M	20 M	Marathon 26.22M
0:09:05	0:18:10	0:27:15	0:36:20	0:45:25	1:30:50	1:59:00	2:16:15	3:01:40	3:58:10
0:09:10	0:18:20	0:27:30	0:36:40	0:45:50	1:31:40	2:00:05	2:17:30	3:03:20	4:00:21
0:09:15	0:18:30	0:27:45	0:37:00	0:46:15	1:32:30	2:01:11	2:18:45	3:05:00	4:02:32
0:09:20	0:18:40	0:28:00	0:37:20	0:46:40	1:33:20	2:02:16	2:20:00	3:06:40	4:04:43
0:09:25	0:18:50	0:28:15	0:37:40	0:47:05	1:34:10	2:03:22	2:21:15	3:08:20	4:06:54
0:09:30	0:19:00	0:28:30	0:38:00	0:47:30	1:35:00	2:04:27	2:22:30	3:10:00	4:09:05
0:09:35	0:19:10	0:28:45	0:38:20	0:47:55	1:35:50	2:05:33	2:23:45	3:11:40	4:11:17
0:09:40	0:19:20	0:29:00	0:38:40	0:48:20	1:36:40	2:06:38	2:25:00	3:13:20	4:13:28
0:09:45	0:19:30	0:29:15	0:39:00	0:48:45	1:37:30	2:07:44	2:26:15	3:15:00	4:15:39
0:09:50	0:19:40	0:29:30	0:39:20	0:49:10	1:38:20	2:08:49	2:27:30	3:16:40	4:17:50
0:09:55	0:19:50	0:29:45	0:39:40	0:49:35	1:39:10	2:09:55	2:28:45	3:18:20	4:20:01
0:10:00	0:20:00	0:30:00	0:40:00	0:50:00	1:40:00	2:11:00	2:30:00	3:20:00	4:22:12
0:10:05	0:20:10	0:30:15	0:40:20	0:50:25	1:40:50	2:12:06	2:31:15	3:21:40	4:24:23
0:10:10	0:20:20	0:30:30	0:40:40	0:50:50	1:41:40	2:13:11	2:32:30	3:23:20	4:26:34
0:10:15	0:20:30	0:30:45	0:41:00	0:51:15	1:42:30	2:14:17	2:33:45	3:25:00	4:28:45
0:10:20	0:20:40	0:31:00	0:41:20	0:51:40	1:43:20	2:15:22	2:35:00	3:26:40	4:30:56
0:10:25	0:20:50	0:31:15	0:41:40	0:52:05	1:44:10	2:16:28	2:36:15	3:28:20	4:33:08
0:10:30	0:21:00	0:31:30	0:42:00	0:52:30	1:45:00	2:17:33	2:37:30	3:30:00	4:35:19
0:10:35	0:21:10	0:31:45	0:42:20	0:52:55	1:45:50	2:18:39	2:38:45	3:31:40	4:37:30
0:10:40	0:21:20	0:32:00	0:42:40	0:53:20	1:46:40	2:19:44	2:40:00	3:33:20	4:39:41
0:10:45	0:21:30	0:32:15	0:43:00	0:53:45	1:47:30	2:20:50	2:41:15	3:35:00	4:41:52
0:10:50	0:21:40	0:32:30	0:43:20	0:54:10	1:48:20	2:21:55	2:42:30	3:36:40	4:44:03
0:10:55	0:21:50	0:32:45	0:43:40	0:54:35	1:49:10	2:23:01	2:43:45	3:38:20	4:46:14
0:11:00	0:22:00	0:33:00	0:44:00	0:55:00	1:50:00	2:24:06	2:45:00	3:40:00	4:48:25
0:11:05	0:22:10	0:33:15	0:44:20	0:55:25	1:50:50	2:25:12	2:46:15	3:41:40	4:50:36
0:11:10	0:22:20	0:33:30	0:44:40	0:55:50	1:51:40	2:26:17	2:47:30	3:43:20	4:52:47
0:11:15	0:22:30	0:33:45	0:45:00	0:56:15	1:52:30	2:27:23	2:48:45	3:45:00	4:54:59
0:11:20	0:22:40	0:34:00	0:45:20	0:56:40	1:53:20	2:28:28	2:50:00	3:46:40	4:57:10
0:11:25	0:22:50	0:34:15	0:45:40	0:57:05	1:54:10	2:29:34	2:51:15	3:48:20	4:59:21
0:11:30	0:23:00	0:34:30	0:46:00	0:57:30	1:55:00	2:30:39	2:52:30	3:50:00	5:01:32
0:11:35	0:23:10	0:34:45	0:46:20	0:57:55	1:55:50	2:31:45	2:53:45	3:51:40	5:03:43
0:11:40	0:23:20	0:35:00	0:46:40	0:58:20	1:56:40	2:32:50	2:55:00	3:53:20	5:05:54
0:11:45	0:23:30	0:35:15	0:47:00	0:58:45	1:57:30	2:33:56	2:56:15	3:55:00	5:08:05
0:11:50	0:23:40	0:35:30	0:47:20	0:59:10	1:58:20	2:35:01	2:57:30	3:56:40	5:10:16
0:11:55	0:23:50	0:35:45	0:47:40	0:59:35	1:59:10	2:36:07	2:58:45	3:58:20	5:12:27
0:12:00	0:24:00	0:36:00	0:48:00	1:00:00	2:00:00	2:37:12	3:00:00	4:00:00	5:14:38
0:12:05	0:24:10	0:36:15	0:48:20	1:00:25	2:00:50	2:38:18	3:01:15	4:01:40	5:16:50
0:12:10	0:24:20	0:36:30	0:48:40	1:00:50	2:01:40	2:39:23	3:02:30	4:03:20	5:19:01
0:12:15	0:24:30	0:36:45	0:49:00	1:01:15	2:02:30	2:40:29	3:03:45	4:05:00	5:21:12
0:12:20	0:24:40	0:37:00	0:49:20	1:01:40	2:03:20	2:41:34	3:05:00	4:06:40	5:23:23
0:12:25	0:24:50	0:37:15	0:49:40	1:02:05	2:04:10	2:42:40	3:06:15	4:08:20	5:25:34
0:12:30	0:25:00	0:37:30	0:50:00	1:02:30	2:05:00	2:43:45	3:07:30	4:10:00	5:27:45
0:12:35	0:25:10	0:37:45	0:50:20	1:02:55	2:05:50	2:44:51	3:08:45	4:11:40	5:29:56
0:12:40	0:25:20	0:38:00	0:50:40	1:03:20	2:06:40	2:45:56	3:10:00	4:13:20	5:32:07
0:12:45	0:25:30	0:38:15	0:51:00	1:03:45	2:07:30	2:47:02	3:11:15	4:15:00	5:34:18
0:12:50	0:25:40	0:38:30	0:51:20	1:04:10	2:08:20	2:48:07	3:12:30	4:16:40	5:36:29
0:12:55	0:25:50	0:38:45	0:51:40	1:04:35	2:09:10	2:49:13	3:13:45	4:18:20	5:38:40
0:13:00	0:26:00	0:39:00	0:52:00	1:05:00	2:10:00	2:50:18	3:15:00	4:20:00	5:40:52